AF316793

My Four Year War
with the US Navy

My Four Year War with the US Navy

V. L. Yeats

ISBN: 979-8-8521-4416-4 (paperback)
ISBN: 979-8-8689-4642-4 (hardcover)

This is a memoir. It contains the author's best recollection of events as they happened. Some names and characteristics may have been changed, some timelines compressed, and some dialog recreated from memory.

Edited by Tyler Yeats

First hardcover edition October 2023.

Contents

My Four Year War with the US Navy

Enlisting

Like most young men in 1941, I had no intention of joining the Navy. World War II had been going on for two years, and the US draft had been operating for over a year. I had a high draft number, and had received a deferment because I worked for the government. That all went away and I became 1-A after the Japanese bombed Pearl Harbor.

The modern generation can remember where they were when Present Kennedy was assassinated. Our generation can remember where we were when Pearl Harbor was bombed. I was playing tennis with Jack Jeffery across from the icehouse in Carrizo Springs, Texas. I was mostly puzzled, and absently minded remarked, where is Pearl Harbor? I was to come to realize not only where it was but also how important the bombing was, and what an effect it would have on the rest of my life and the lives of millions of other Americans.

In anticipation of the draft, I had previously attempted to enlist in the Army Air Corps as a pilot, or in some other capacity. I took the entrance exam along with 90 other aspiring pilots, and finished up in the top four. Great!! I was just what the Army Air Corps was looking for. An officer took me in hand, shook his head when he saw the glasses I was wearing, and said, "Let's save time and run you down to take the eye examination." It did not take long to find out that I had the depth perception of a near-sighted warthog—so much for my brief career with the Air Force.

With this experience behind me, I decided to just report for physical examination when called by the draft board, and let the army have its way with me. Putting my affairs in order was not very difficult for me to do. I was 22 years old, unmarried, had no encumbrances, and very little personal property. I made arrangements to store my 1936 Plymouth at my sister's house. Cars became greatly in demand later on during the war, but at the beginning with so many young men entering the service, most men sold their cars at sacrifice prices. One of the few smart things I have ever planned was the idea to store my car until after the war. I jacked it up on blocks, put a canvas over it, and gave the tires to my brother-in-law.

1936 Plymouth Coupe, *Esso*

I reported to the draft board for induction when requested to do so. The draft board secretary was Beth Stone, a girl who was in my high school graduating class. I told her I had a few things to attend to, and would return in a few minutes. When I returned, the inductees were climbing aboard the bus. I reported to Beth, and she smiled and said that they always called a few extra people in order to be sure of filling their quota, and that their quota for this time had already been filled. So I got a 30-day reprieve. Beth didn't say so, but I think she did it on purpose. But she did tell me that I would be #1 on the next quota.

It was during this 30-day reprieve that I ran into my cousin, J. L. Speer. He told me that rather than to be drafted into the army, he was going to enlist in the Navy, and hoped to be given a petty officer's rating of cook 3rd class. I was not looking forward to joining the army, and the idea of joining the Navy sounded a lot better. So I went with him to San Antonio to talk to the Navy recruiting officer.

The Navy recruiting office was a place where pandemonium reigned. It was filled with harried officers, busy chiefs, and yeomen knee deep in enlistment forms. From this swirl of activity I finally staggered away with a promise of a 3rd class storekeeper rating and with orders to report back to San Antonio on March 6th, 1942, for duty. Upon what trivial events are the directions of our lives determined. My cousin J. L and I reported as ordered on that fateful 6th day of March, 1942, and along with half a hundred

Dewey Speer and son J. L.

other callow youths, raised our right hands and swore to defend our country against all enemies, both foreign and domestic, for the duration of the war and six months.

We were put on a train that dropped us off in Houston, and there were put in a hotel with a mounting number of other recruits. The next morning we climbed aboard a train bound for California. Traveling during the war was almost exclusively by railroad since both gasoline and automobile tires were rationed and in short supply. I had not done any traveling by train since

I was a small child, but I was to do a lot of it during the next four years. The long trip to California was a novelty to me. Fellow passengers on the long trip with me across the country were a mixture of recruits, men from all branches of the services, their families, and other civilians. This loaded caravan took three days to wend its way to San Diego, our final destination.

Boot Camp

During peacetime, the Navy required six months to turn raw recruits into sailors. The procedures of wartime reduced the time to six weeks. There is nothing like the humiliation heaped upon recruits at a Navy boot camp. I think it is worse than other service recruit training, but maybe that is because the Navy experience is the only one which I observed first hand. Perhaps only the uniforms are different. In any event, when we arrived in camp, some tough first class bosun mate gave us a lecture telling us to throw away all whisky, condoms, dirty pictures, and other useful civilian items into a large barrel. I am sure he went through it and picked out what he wanted later.

We were given shots in all sorts of places to protect us against diseases we had never heard of. Then came the issuing of clothing the likes of which I had never seen before, pants with a multitude of buttons on the front, a flap which folded down on the wrong side for practical use, and worst of all, with no pockets. This was topped off with two hats, neither of which was fit to wear, and a sissy-looking silk neckerchief. The only reasonable piece of haberdashery in the lot was a pea coat whose versatility and warmth made up for a lot of other deficiencies, and the dungarees. And, of course, we all received the traditional peeled-look hair cut.

Our actual clothing allowance, as I best remember it, was the following: one suit of dress blues, two suits of undress blues, two sets of whites, two sets of dungarees, four sets of underwear, four pairs of socks, one pair of black shoes, one pair of boots, one pea coat, one neckerchief, two white hats, one flat hat, one mattress, two mattress covers, one pillow, two pillow cases, one sewing kit, two sets of laundry cords, one ditty bag, one blanket, one hammock, a sea bag, and a Bluejacket Manual.

Some of these items require additional information. The ditty bag is a small canvas sack with a drawstring, and is about the size of a football. It is to hold all the small items a sailor might need including all the items need for male hygiene and titivations. The hammock, a traditional Navy item, although seldom used to sleep in, served another useful function. All a sailor's clothing packed in his sea bag fits nicely into the rolled up and lashed together

Boot Camp, San Diego

mattress, pillow, and blanket. This compact, one-piece unit could be carried by a healthy bluejacket when and if he were transferred or moved. I know I carried mine many places.

The Bluejacket Manuel was the sailors' Bible. It contained innumerable explanations of naval procedures and seamanship information. It also explained what a sailor should and should not do while in the Navy. It was a seaman's reference book. One thing you soon noticed at boot camp was that you had to learn a nautical vocabulary. Other than the obvious fore and aft, port and starboard, deck and overhead, ladders and passageways, topside and below, you had to interpret such expressions as "Abaft the starboard beam," and "Belay that last order," and "Tighten those tit gripes." You also learned that the only rope aboard ships is the bell rope. All others are lines. You soon became used to daily exhortation by the bosun over the loudspeakers following wailing of his pipe, such as "Sweepers man you brooms, a clean sweep down fore and aft," or "Now hear this. All working parties report to their duty station," or "The smoking lamp is lit," and so on.

The Navy also has a strange way of telling time. As in all other military

units, the day consists of twenty-four hours, and is read from one to twenty-four. But Navy time is related to four-hour watches. Time is recorded every half-hour by ringing the appropriate number on the ship's bell. After eight bells, the ringing sequence starts over to record the four-hour watches. You have, then, six four-hour watches, and six sequences of half-hour bells until a total of eight bells have been rung. At that time you start a new sequence of bells, and the beginning of a new watch.

Boot camp time was filled with chores, many of which were boring, but all of them had a purpose. As in all military organizations, we had to perform all sorts of mundane chores, such as making up our bunks and keeping our barracks clean. Except that we did not have barracks. Due to the wartime rush and the enormous number of new recruits, rows of tents were strung out on part of the parade grounds.

We seemed to spend an inordinate amount of time learning to march and perform drills. This I did not enjoy; in fact, I hated it. It did not seem to me to be an important part of naval instruction. But nevertheless, I did it along with the rest of the recruits. I was never very good at it, probably because I did not like it, but like the rest, I endured, and learned to obey the drillmaster's instructions. We all pulled guard duty, mostly for the purpose of learning how, as most of the time we might be guarding something as important as a clothes line. But the worst part was the chore of having to put on our canvas leggings. These had to be laced up, which was quite a chore. (I forgot to mention that the leggings were part of our clothing issue.)

We had our own laundry shed where we washed our clothes with scrub brushes on wooden planks — just a cut above beating them with a rock in a primitive river. Once clean, clothes were tied with cloth stops (small bits of cord) to the clothesline. This was done with a square knot of course. And all articles must be tied in their own group. No socks allowed in with the dungarees.

Regimentation was everything. We spent some time learning how to tie knots. I still remember square knots, half hitches, clove hitches, timber hitches, bowlines, and bowlines on a bight. But I never learned to splice ropes. (Excuse me, I meant lines.) But I learned what a fid was.

We had many other duties as well. Mess duty was foremost. Probably the worst duty was head patrol. As mentioned previously, we had no barracks and were quartered in tents. Our mess hall, laundry room, and heads were temporary wooden buildings. Our head was a simple wooden building lined with galvanized troughs that were hooked up so that water could flow through them. Valves controlled the flow of water and could be shut off when not in use. The tops of the troughs were fitted with wooden caps so that one could sit relatively comfortably while performing the customary chore. When the head was empty, all the water could be cut off. As people begin to come into the head, it was the head masters job to regulate the flow of water to remove the effluent. He was issued a broomstick with which to prod the reluctant turds, and speed them on their way. His duty was also to conserve space and water. This meant persuading, or even demanding that sailors sit side by side, like the clothing on the clothesline rather than seeking privacy across the room.

Most people do not like to sit in a cubicle next to some one in a restroom. Imagine twenty or thirty young recruits sitting buttock-to-buttock and straining all at the same time. The pungent aroma produced as a result of the combined efforts of so many virile young bodies was enough to stun a rhinoceros.

Every morning after chow we reported for muster. After answering our name at roll call, our Chief reported to the company officer who in turn reported to the commanding officer. The daily announcements were reported to us, and then we were read a portion of Rocks and Shoals, or a list of naughty things you must not do while in the Navy. It worried me that a number of these no-noes were followed by the solemn pronouncement "and the penalty is death." I took extreme pains no to commit any such dire acts.

Our instructors were not officers, but chief petty officers. Ordinarily they would have been bosun mates, and they did hold this rating. But they were just as much a bunch of recruits as we. Mostly they were ex-athletic coaches and physical instructors, all young, and all landlubbers.

I remember my first payday in the Navy. I don't remember how much I made as an Sk 3rd class, but I think it was about 35 dollars a month. Payday was the first day of the month, and as with all the military services, payment was in cash. We lined up according to the alphabet (I was at the tail end, of course). We were herded around by a bunch of superannuated chiefs with hash marks weighing down their arms (they had been called back from retirement). I think their job was to bluster, yell, and glower, and otherwise intimidate us. Actually I believe they envied the scintillating vitality generated by such a group of young people. And then it was the paymaster's job to make scathing remarks about incipient storekeepers who couldn't spell "forty."

Terminal Island

After completing our boot training, we were transferred to barracks to wait for assignments to permanent duty stations. This we looked forward to with considerable enthusiasm. Surely our new assignments would be better than boot camp. But our assignments presented a problem. It seems that in their enthusiasm to attract volunteers to the Navy, they had signed up too many storekeepers and yeomen. Yes, they would need us in time. But the time was not yet — it takes time to build up the strong military system that now was in the making in America. In the meantime, there we were, eager and willing to serve, but there were not enough assignments for our numbers. In order to fill other vital ranks, they offered to retrain us excess storekeepers and yeomen in new fields in which there were shortages. I was all set to go to torpedo man school.

Why not? I was short and heavy set, and good at weight lifting. However, wiser heads prevailed, and the retraining programs were cancelled. Instead, all the storekeepers were sent to Terminal Island to a storekeeper school. This involved another train trip, but this time, a much shorter one. It was time to load up our bags, lash up our bedding in our hammock, tie it altogether in a neat bundle, board the train, and take a nice slow trip up the coast to Terminal Island, which is near Long Beach.

Terminal Island consisted of docking facilities for fishing boats, fish canneries, and a Federal prison. It was a pleasant enough place despite the grim, forbidding appearance of the fortress-like buildings, and the lingering smell of fish emanating from the canneries.

The prison was then empty of federal prisoners, but did contain some Navy prisoners, and there was a small contingent of marines to guard them. After a while you got used to seeing marines with sawed-off shotguns escorting Navy prisoners in double time across the parade ground. It came as a shock to me to discover that all sailors were not patriotic volunteers dedicated to saving the world for democracy.

Many were simply paying the penalty for being AWOL, others for over-staying a leave, but sadly, many were there because they stole from Uncle Sam. These were for the main part, cooks, storekeepers, and paymasters. Why these people? Because they were the people who were responsible for the food, the merchandise, and the money for the Navy, and some few of them could not resist the temptation to abuse that responsibility. But still even more sadly, some were in prison because they were homosexuals. The military policy may now be don't ask, don't tell, but at that time the policy was don't be, and homosexuality was strictly verboten, and a sure cause for a dishonorable discharge — no pun intended.

In spite of this grim background, the time I spent at Terminal Island was one of the happiest of my naval tenure. I volunteered for mess duty, because once your duties were finished, you were free to go on liberty every day. Long Beach was only a short hop from Los Angles and the fleshpots of Hollywood. In San Diego, when you went on liberty, you were drowned in a sea of bluejackets. San Diego was a relatively small town at that time, and the servicemen almost outnumbered the civilians. On the other hand, Los Angles was one of the largest cities in the US, and there were relatively few servicemen stationed in the area. Remember also that this was in the early part of the war, and sailors were welcomed as the saviors of their country, and nothing was too good for them.

The USO, Stage Door Canteen, or Bundles for Bluejackets always had spare tickets for stage shows, nightclubs, and even burlesque shows. Most nightclubs had live entertainment as well. It was even difficult to pay for a bottle of beer in a pub. These Zigfield Follies types of shows no longer exist, but there were several of them in Los Angles at that time. One night I even helped put on the floorshow at the Florentine Gardens.

This was quite different from the nightlife in San Diego, where you were always knee-deep in bluejackets wherever you went. There was one exception to this. This was the burlesque house on 4th and F streets in San Diego. That was the only sensible place to go for a sailor, and they put on the best burlesque show on the West Coast. They had beautiful girls and their comedians were really funny. I can still remember some of the jokes of comedian Say No More Joe. And very sensibly next door was a hole in the wall where they served nothing but German fried potatoes. When I returned to San Diego forty years later, I found to my horror that they had torn down the burlesque house and replaced it with a mall. This cannot be considered progress. Rest in peace Say No More Joe.

All good things eventually come to an end, and so it happened to the storekeeper school on Terminal Island. Having finished our instructions at the school, we were herded onto a train and shipped back to San Diego to the Receiving Station there.

Setting Sail

Receiving Stations are the pits in the Navy. They accept you because they have to, but nobody wants you. You aren't ship's company, and you are in a state of limbo. And after Hollywood, San Diego was pretty dull, even with its burlesque show.

After a few weeks of being in limbo, a number of us storekeeper were transferred to the Destroyer Base. We were still in San Diego, but we belonged to some one and were ship's company. We were assigned to the Landing Craft Depot, which was a new organization set up to provide for the needs of the amphibious forces being built for the coming invasion of the Japanese held islands in the Pacific. My stay at the Destroyer Base was a short one. I had been in the Navy for eight months, and it was now time to move on, and this time overseas.

Our team was composed of ten 3rd class storekeepers, two chiefs, and our leader, Commander Bean. Once again it was time to pick my bed and baggage combination and walk to the train station. This time we traveled all the way to San Francisco. Once there, I again picked up my familiar possessions and carried them aboard the HMS Sommelsdijk, a new Dutch diesel motor ship, leased to the US by the Dutch government in exile. The ship had been fortunate enough to be at sea when Hitler marched into Holland, and the Captain and crew wisely decided not to return to their homeport.

We moved down the coast to Port Hueneme to pick up cargo and also a shipload of CBs. Here I had the last liberty in the States for a long time, and that was by accident. Our commanding officer was Commander George Bean, who had been the owner of a large automotive parts company in Los Angles. He must have been in the Naval Reserve to come into the Navy with that rank. I met a lot of characters while I was in the Navy, but this guy was unique. If I had to characterize him, I would say that he reminded me of General Patton, another guy named George. He gave liberty to half the storekeepers for the first night that we would be in town, and this did not include me. But he said that we would have to supply one person for shore patrol duty, and that could be me. So I strapped on those accursed canvas leggings, headed for the shore patrol station, and reported in.

The Officer in Charge took one look at me in my leggings and said to me curtly, "Get out. We have our own shore patrol units, and we don't need any help from you." So I took off those despised leggings and enjoyed liberty with the rest of the crew. The fact that they didn't need me somewhat upset Commander Bean, as it didn't make him look too good.

We stayed there two days loading cargo, and became acquainted with people in the nearby town of Oxnard. Of all the towns and cities I visited in California, I was most impressed with this one. I made the observation that if I ever moved to California, this would be where I would want to live. Apparently a lot of other servicemen felt the same way, and moved there after the war was over.

The next day we shoved off, loaded down with cargo, even on our decks, which were loaded with lumber and trucks. Part of our cargo consisted of several hundred CBs. They were a fierce looking bunch with unshaved faces and shaven heads, and sporting fresh tattoos. They were mostly from the East Coast, and a high percentage of them claimed to be from Brooklyn.

MS Sommelsdijk

The Sommelsdijk was a well-built, modern diesel motor ship, and it is a good thing that she was, because in the middle of the Pacific Ocean we ran into a typhoon which generated winds of over 90 knots. We lost none of the crew or passengers, but a considerable part of our deck cargo of trucks and lumber went over the side during the storm. We shipped in some water, most of which ended up swirling around in the galley. We were fortunate to be able to have Spam sandwiches for a couple of days. The CBs didn't mind the change in cuisine, as they spent most of the time throwing up in the head. The person most affected by the storm was a poor seaman who was on watch in the crow's nest and was unable to come down for twenty-four hours because of the intensity of the storm. The only other excitement on the trip was our introduction to King Neptune at the celebration of the crossing of the equator. We also had the distinction of passing by Christmas Island on Christmas day.

New Caledonia

In due time near the end of the year 1942, we arrived at our destination of Nouméa, New Caledonia. I had never heard of New Caledonia, and it certainly is not the most well known place in the world. So perhaps a little historical background is in order.

French explorers as pirates and privateers began to challenge the Spanish in the Pacific in the 1600s, but it was the explorer Louis Antoine de Bougainville who opened up the Pacific for the French. His voyages set the pattern for other French explorers. After Napoleon's defeat in Europe, everything changed for the French, as his dreams of conquest collapsed at Waterloo. But although defeated in Europe, France hoped to keep England at bay in the Pacific. In order to accomplish this, it was necessary for them to maintain a naval presence in the Pacific, and this required naval bases. One such base was set up in Nouméa, New Caledonia.

One of the tasks of such a Navy was to provide protection for the Catholic missionaries. These missionaries considered their work of evangelism a political check against Protestantism, which was identified with English interests. Territorial acquisition began in 1853, and annexation followed soon afterwards. A penal colony was established in 1863, just as the English had done in Australia, and the penal system remained the cornerstone of colonial society in New Caledonia for the next thirty years. The city of Nouméa slowly developed as a military base and administration center for the area, and thousands of prisoners were located there.

The original inhabitants of the island were Melanesian in origin and were called Kanaks. They resented being pushed off their land by the encroaching Europeans, and in 1878 they revolted and attacked the colonists. It was cowboys and Indians all over again. The rebellion was squashed and actually freed up additional land for the colonists. Immigration continued from France, but growth was slow. Mining became important with the discovery of nickel, and was backed financially by Baron Rothschild. By the turn of the century, New Caledonia had become an important producer of this strategic metal. Immigration of Orientals became necessary to work as miners, and they were re-

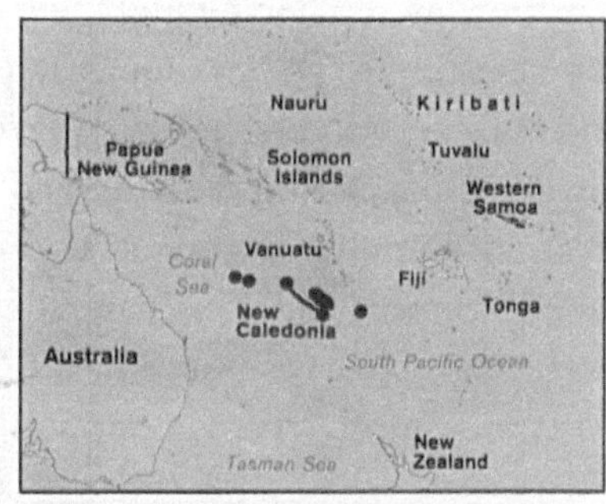

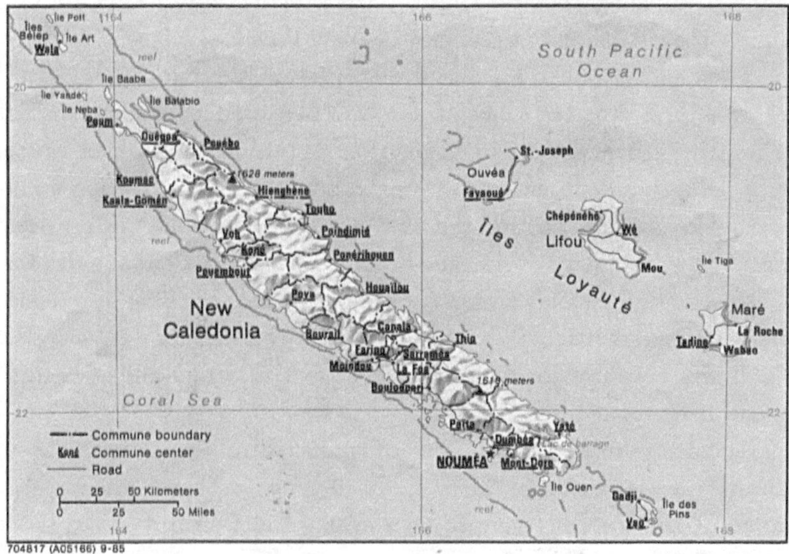

ported to be better miners than the Kanaks. Eventually there were more exotic workers than there were European workers.

From 1887 until 1947, Kanaks were subjected to social and political discrimination. Despite this, the Kanaks actually participated in both WWI and WWII. New Caledonia as well as the rest of the Pacific was thrust suddenly into the world conflict. The islanders sided with De Gaulle and the Free French. The United States military command decided to transform Nouméa into a forward military base, and in the space of three years, thousands of US troops passed through New Caledonia, changing it forever.

I still have a faded copy of the military newspaper of WWII called *Yank*, which has an article on the peaceful occupation of Nouméa and some of the effects this inundation of foreign troops had on the people and their culture.

We at the Landing Force Equipment Depot as we were called, did not have many occasions to go to Nouméa, and we were pretty much isolated on the island of Île Nou across the bay. We were allowed on liberty, and occasionally we would cross over to the mainland and spend a few hours in Nouméa for recreation. But after you strolled along the few streets, admired the petite Javanese women, had your haircut by a woman barber (if you were very daring, you could have it singed), and drank a lemonade at one of the sidewalk cafes, it was time to return to camp. Exotic, very pretty, but not very exciting.

We disembarked from the good ship Sommelsdijk, shouldered our belongings, and hauled them to a nearby truck, which took us on a tour of Nouméa, the capital and largest city of New Caledonia. It was a colorful town, filled with people dressed in strange costumes. I quickly noticed that there were three different kinds of people. There were the Europeans who were mostly French, dressed in conventional clothing; the oriental women, mostly petite Javanese, dressed in long robes, and often carrying a child in a sash-like contraption; and the natives, the Kanaks, black as the ace of spades. The men were powerful, and beautifully built, but rather fierce looking. They had kinky hair, which was often bleached to an outlandish reddish-blonde. They were magnificent specimens, but the women were just specimens. It was here that for the first time I saw the beauty and smelled the aroma of fringe pang blossoms.

We finally were put on a boat and conducted to what was to become our home for the next year, the island of Île Nou, just across the bay from Nouméa. There we were dumped on a dock — fourteen bewildered sailors, two officers, two chiefs, and ten bluejacket storekeepers. We were to get to know each other very well in time.

Landing Force Equipment Depot

Our commanding officer was Lt. Colonel George Bean. We were also assigned a Lieutenant Junior grade, whose name I cannot remember. There
were two chief petty officers assigned to as well, Chief Horn, and another
whose name I cannot remember. The rest were storekeepers 3/c, and besides
myself were:

- Kaler E. Bowl from Kansas, who forever afterwards would be called
  Soup. He told us he had a sister nicknamed Sugar. Soup was our Mr.
  Personality, an All American boy who got along with everybody, and
  whom everybody liked.

- Bernardi was a person of Italian extraction from San Francisco. Every
  outfit in the service had a Bernardi. He was the sharp guy who knew
  everyone, knew all the angles, and was inclined to cut corners if it was
  necessary.

- Markow was from Los Angles. He was a dark, brooding, Mediter-
  ranean type, in love with a girl who was stringing him along, and he
  worried about it the whole time I knew him.

- Leitz was from St Louis. He was blonde, clean cut, trusting, always
  had on a clean suit of dungarees, and was really a nice guy.

- Zeller was from Chicago, and in his early thirties, somewhat older than
  most of the rest of us. He was very reticent, and seldom volunteered
  any conversation that was not required. He was undoubtedly of German ancestry although he never said so. He was rather clumsy in his
  movements, and was built like a beer-barrel.

- Kopp was another mid-westerner. He was also rather quiet and undis-
  tinguished, and usually had little to say. Perhaps it was just such a char-
  acteristic that keeps me from remembering much about him.

- Clyde was from Wewoka, Oklahoma, and had been a bookkeeper for an oil company. He also was in his thirties. He had a keen sense of humor, and the crew, except for the person who happened to be the butt of his joke always enjoyed his repartee. It is strange that he is the only one in the group who was usually called by his first name.

- Pop was the nickname for the oldest member of our crew. He also was from the Middle West, had a portly build, smoked a pipe constantly, and wore a crew cut that was going slightly bald. He probably knew more about the parts business and warehousing than all the rest of us put together.

- I have racked my brain, but have been unable to come with the name of the last of the crew. He was blonde, in his early thirties in age, was well educated, well liked, and extremely liberal in his views. He was from Los Angeles. We had many discussions and enjoyed each other's company, but I cannot tell you his name.

  I will mention a story he told me which was indicative of the poverty of the times. He said that while on a hunting trip with a well off friend it, was necessary for his friend to answer a call of nature. Afterwards they discovered that neither of them had any paper of any kind. Out of necessity his friend used the only thing he could think of, which happened to be a couple dollar bills. My friend, who was not so well off, suffered untold agony. He wanted to go back after those bills, but pride prevented him.

None of the ten of us were married. That some of us were older than the average sailor may be attributed to the fact that we had all came into the Navy with a rating, and had some experience.

We were not aware of it at the time, but Île Nou was to be our home for the next year. There was already a small naval station on the island, and we took over some of the existing buildings and soon had a small office and several warehouses for parts. We became, in effect, a forward extension of the amphibious depot in San Diego. We called ourselves The Landing Force Equipment Depot, and our Navy code designation was Epic 93.

For the first few months we were busy preparing our warehouses and stowing the material we had brought with us from San Diego. I spent most of my time in the office we had set up, typing requisitions for new equipment.

A typical LCM (Landing Craft Mechanized) in the Marianas

We were soon able to begin supplying the amphibious force, which was what we had been sent to do.

Most of the ships we supplied were former passenger ships from the President Line, such as the Jackson, the Coolidge, and the Adams. These former cruise ships had been pressed into service by the Navy and converted into amphibious attack vessels. Amphibious ships such as these were shuttled halfway around the world. They were first used in North Africa, then in Alaska, and now in the Pacific to begin the island hopping campaign beginning with Guadalcanal in the Solomon Islands. In time, we began to accumulate our own amphibious fleet. For a time, I was in charge of this miniature Navy anchored out in the bay. It was a welcomed change from working in the office. I had my own LCP (Landing Craft Personnel). I had never piloted a power driven boat in my life, but learning was fun.

We were housed in tents lined up in rows on terraces cut into the side of a hill overlooking the bay. These were reasonably comfortable for sleeping, except when it rained and water ran down the hill and under our tents. We slept on army cots and kept all our clothes in our sea bags. It was not long before wooden crates were converted into usable furniture. We did not spend much time in our tents except when we were sleeping. We were four in a tent. Soup Bole and I shared the same tent and had cots next to each other. He had

Landing Craft Personnel (LCP)

a habit of talking in his sleep, and sometimes would get up and walk in his sleep. It happened so frequently that we would actually bet and give odds on whether Soup would walk that night or not. One night he walked outside the tent when it was raining and woke up wet and cold with muddy feet.

After establishing ourselves on Île Nou, life settled down to routine work, and it sometimes seemed as if we stagnating in the backwaters of the war. I stayed there a year, and most of what I did was not important enough to be reported here. There are a few things that remain stuck in my mind; some are trivial, some important, some amusing, and some tragic. Île Nou was an elongated Island whose presence created the wonderful harbor of Noumea.

We were at one end of the island, but if we were off duty, we were free to wander about. Soup Bole was my tent mate, and a good friend as well. We often spent some time exploring other parts of the island. Soup, being the gregarious person he was, made friends wherever he went. There was a prison near the center of the island, and he made friends with the son of the warden of the prison. We were interested to learn that they had the death penalty in New Caledonia, and being French, they used the guillotine for executions. There was a guillotine at the prison, and they had occasion to use it while we were on the island. A Javanese had killed his wife, and he had been sentenced to be executed for the crime. The warden of the prison invited us to witness the execution, but we declined the invitation.

I mentioned earlier that one of my duties was to be coxswain of our boat. We had a major inspection by the CO of the Naval Station, who happened to be a four-striper. Afterward, Commander Bean, always out to make a good impression with the Navy brass, offered him a ride across the bay in our boat. Bad decision. Half way across the bay for no apparent reason whatsoever, the boat conked out. We drifted about aimlessly while I frantically tried to restart the engine. No dice. We finally managed to tie up to a buoy in the middle of the bay, where a passing boat rescued the by now grumpy four-striper and a humiliated Commander Bean. Guess who stayed with the recalcitrant boat until after dark and was finally towed back to the base in disgrace. There is no defense against such a catastrophe. Never mind that the engine had been running perfectly. Never mind that I was not a mechanic and could not be expected to diagnose engine trouble in the middle of the bay, let alone repair it. Shoot the messenger who brings bad tidings. After that experience, I knew how Dr. Mudd, that unfortunate but innocent man who unwittingly befriended the man who shot Lincoln, felt. We both had the misfortune to be at the wrong place at the wrong time. His name was Mudd, as was mine, through no fault of my own.

Commander Bean was a remarkable man. I think that I mentioned that he shared many of the characteristics of General Patton. The story is told that once the General became upset because his forward progress was slowed by the presence of a swiftly flowing stream. He wanted his troops to swim across the water, but they held back because they feared that they would drown. General Patton dived into the water, swam across, and then swam back and said to his troops, "See, it was easy." A similar incident happened with Commander Bean. Some sailors were trying to rig some lines on a boat at high tide. The Commander was shouting orders to them from the shore, and becoming impatient with their lack of success, dove into the water, swam to the boat, and quickly secured the lines. Again the words, "See, It was easy."

Commander Bean and I had our disagreements over many things. There was the time he wanted me to be a bartender at the new officers club they were building at the top of the hill above the camp. It was to be a quiet retreat where the brass could carouse in seclusion. Unfortunately, it was in our back yard, and it didn't help our morale any when we had to watch the officers stroll up the hill accompanied by nurses from the hospital from Noumea. To see this was particularly galling to the enlisted sailors. I still remember watching a drunken four-striper urinate off the pier while a bevy of embarrassed nurses pretended not to notice and looked the other way. I told Commander Bean in a respectful way that I had not joined the Navy to tend bar and that I did not believe that tending bar at the officers club was an effective way to fight the Japanese. In any event, I did not get a promotion I would have gotten had I taken the job, but it gave me a righteous feeling, and I still feel good about it over fifty years later.

Soup was the first of us to be promoted, and probably rightly so. Still, it is interesting how it came about. He didn't do it by tending bar, but by stealing a load of plywood. Plywood was like gold in the South Pacific. We needed it very badly for shelving. Dress was always very informal, and most people wore dungarees. The only way you knew ones rank was by the insignia they wore. Soup borrowed a Chief's hat, commandeered a boat and a working party, cruised to the Naval Supply Depot, searched until he found a pile of plywood, and started the working party loading it. When the harried store-keeper came over for the requisition, Soup stalled him with double-talked, walked with him over to the office, and made the excuse that he had to go to the head. Chief Soup and the load of plywood disappeared simultaneously.

Admiral Halsey called the sailors at Epic (Noumea) the biggest gang of thieves since Ali Baba. We could have gotten the plywood in time by regular requisitions, but Commander Bean did not want to wait the time it would take to get the material by going through regular channels. I once jokingly asked him if he was related to Judge Roy Bean, the Law West of the Pecos. With out batting an eyelash he stated, "He was one of us." He may very well have been.

Navy Operations

Plywood was not the only thing stolen from the supply base. The stealing did not take place for the usual reason. Everyone had plenty of money, there was just very little that you could buy. Therefore what could not be bought was sometimes stolen. Some things that a sailor thought he needed but could not buy accidentally got mixed in with requisitioned material. Once a full case of Optimo cigars mysteriously showed up. These were wonderful cigars in round tins of twenty-five, and a case totaled 600 cigars. Every sailor in camp had a big stogie in his mouth for weeks. But the cigars were not the most exciting item to show up. Some unknown sailors purloined a five-gallon can of alcohol. To their disgust they discovered that it was denatured.

You must remember that alcohol is strictly verboten aboard US ships. This applies to shore stations as well, and even in the States we were restricted to 3.2 beer on the base. We certainly did not have any spirits at Epic 93. Alcohol, when necessary for use aboard ship, such as in ships binnacles, is adulterated so as to make it unfit to drink, and is bright red in color. It was called torpedo juice, and all sailors knew better than to drink it. Desperately thirsty sailors had been known to filter it through a loaf of bread to remove the adulterant. This crude method of refinement universally fails to remove all the contamination, and the result is usually a sick bunch of sailors spending time in the brig.

We didn't wish to risk a disaster such as that. "Look fellows," I told them. "What the Navy added to the alcohol can be taken out, but it has to be done in the right manner. Science can find such a way. What we need is a still." A five-gallon can and a roll of copper tubing appeared as if by magic, an electrician was recruited to do the soldering, a Pyrex bottle and rubber tubing completed the ensemble, and before you could say "Jack Daniels" three times, we had a still operating.

It was crude but effective. Aside from catching fire a couple of times, it worked very efficiently. We forgot that alcohol boils at a lower point than water, and we had created too hot a fire. We eventually ended up with over two gallons of potent Everclear. Mixed with grapefruit juice that the galley cheerfully provided, we produced a drink that seemed innocuous, but was in fact deadly. The result was a sudden bunch of drunken sailors and horrendous hangovers in the morning.

Quarters the following morning were a dreary mess. Commander Bean knew something was going on, but we kept our secret, and insofar as I know, he never knew what had happened. Everyone agreed that it was a marvelous party, and it was the principal topic of conversation for weeks afterward.

Another event that sticks in my mind as a memory of New Caledonia was the tragedy of the ammunition explosion on the loading docks at the Naval Station in Noumea. I was standing in the doorway of one of our warehouses with my back toward Noumea across the bay, when shock waves from a tremendous explosion begin flapping my trouser legs. I was startled, turned around to look across the bay, and saw there a tremendous column of fire and smoke mushrooming into the air. We never knew for sure exactly what happened, but scuttlebutt (Navy gossip) was rampant. A lot of ammunition went up in smoke, and there was tremendous damage and serious loss of life.

Clyde Moss, who has been a friend of mine for years, was a Chief pharmacist mate in Noumea at the time of the explosion and was involved in the rescue work. His remark to me was, "You should be glad that you were not involved in it." We often reminisce about adventures and life in Noumea. Unfortunately we did not know each other at that time, and it was only years later that we discovered that we were both in Noumea at the same time.

Another event that broke the monotony of life on Île Nou was the discovery of the boat. Many Noumeans had small boats which they used for fishing or just getting around the bay. One of these boats drifted ashore one morning at high tide, and I claimed it as salvage rights and pulled it ashore. It had no sail and no oars, but we acquired some oars and had a lot of fun rowing around in the bay. Every one used it from time to time, but it was my boat by right of discovery. After several weeks we decided no one was going to claim it, so we cleaned it up, repaired it, and painted it, and she became a first class boat. She suffered some damage when a tank lighter drifted into her and cracked a few ribs. Commander Bean, who was standing by when it happened, used some words that would have been a credit for a bosun, but were perhaps somewhat unbecoming for an officer.

Despite whatever differences we might have had, he thought the boat was a great idea. Some of his benevolent feeling for it evaporated when one of the crew went fishing in it, tied up to a barge, got towed out to sea, and had difficulty getting back. Some months later a Frenchman came looking for a missing boat. Since we had painted it and policed it up, we were not convinced that it was his boat. It seems that sometimes when sailors were stranded they would "borrow" a boat, and abandon it when they got where they wished to go. Again, Commander Bean came to our aid, and refused to give up the boat. When it came time for us to go to Guadalcanal, he tried to get permission to load the boat aboard the ship to take it with us, but was unable to do so. I said goodbye to the boat reluctantly when it was time to leave, but managed to sell it for fifty bucks.

When we first came to Noumea, the battle for the island of Guadalcanal was underway. When the island was secured, it was time for Landing Craft Equipment Depot to move up. An advance crew was sent ahead of time to set up shop. I was not a part of that group, and the bulk of our crew did not leave for Guadalcanal until several weeks afterwards. I wish I could remember the name of the ship we sailed on. I know it was one from the President Line, but I do not remember which one. I only remember that I spent most of the daylight time playing blackjack on a hatch cover, and that I did not win.

Guadalcanal

Before WWII, Guadalcanal was certainly not a place I knew anything about. Perhaps as with Noumea, it might be well to consider some of the history of the island. The Solomon Islands, of which Guadalcanal is one, are a part of the Ring of Fire of the Pacific. Here is found the intersection of the Oceanic and the Indo-Australian plates. The movement between these plates results in the occurrence of many earthquakes and occasional volcanic action. I felt the vibration of earthquakes several times during the year I was on the island. There are three active volcanoes on land and several submarine volcanoes as well in the Guadalcanal chain. The islands are in the form of a scattered double chain.

Many of the islands are rugged, heavily forested mountains, while others are flat-lying coral atolls. Guadalcanal is one of the larger islands of this group and contains the highest peak, Mount Popomanaseu. The mountains are composed of igneous rock and consist of many steep-sided, narrow valleys covered by a rain forest. The coastline consists of sandy beaches, lagoons, and mangrove swamps. Henderson Airfield lies on flat outwash plains between the mountains. It was of tremendous strategic importance.

Westward migration of the Polynesians reached the outer edge of the Solomons between 1200 and 1600 AD. They found the islands already settled by Melanesians... apparently this preexisting population was either destroyed or absorbed. Spanish exploration began in the 1500s, while the English were not there until the middle 1700s. Whalers were known to have been in the area by 1800. Visiting sailors of all nations brought new diseases to the inhabitants that were a catastrophe to a population that had no resistance to these strange diseases.

Sandalwood traders followed in the footsteps of the whalers. They came to be hated by the islanders because of the bad treatment received from them. This justified hatred became so intense that the natives would kill any white man that they saw, and the Solomon Islands gained the reputation of being the most dangerous place in the Pacific. Introduction of firearms produced an explosive growth of head hunting and a labor recruiting development called "black birding." It is estimated that over 30,000 Solomon Islanders were taken to Australia to work on the sugar plantations.

In 1893 Great Britain proclaimed a protectorate over the Islands. This was done principally to stop head hunting, cannibalism, and black birding. An able administrator named Charles Woodford was appointed who laid the foundation for organized government. He retired in 1915. Education and health concerns were left largely to the missionaries. Conflicts resulted between the various groups due to the different versions of Christianity as presented by different churches. Island traditions changed because the missionaries condemned many of the native customs.

Population declined due to the diseases introduced by the Europeans. Rebellions by the natives occurred, but were subdued by 1928. The 1930s represented a period of relative calm, but this was shattered by the invasion of the islands by the Japanese in 1942. Their treatment of the natives was less than exemplary, with the result that there was almost complete rejection of the Japanese by the natives due to their cruelty and destruction of property. They occupied the island of Tulagi, which contained the only city in the area, and began to build an airfield on the island of Guadalcanal located just across the bay. Large scale landing of troops by the United States set the stage for land and sea battles to follow.

The Landing Force Equipment Depot warehouse and offices were located on Lunga Point on the beach, and was one of the invasion points for the American troops. When we landed there, our advance group that had been on the island for several weeks met us. They considered themselves to be grizzled veterans, having been inflicted with such inconveniences such as exploding ammunition dumps and Bed Check Charlie. The predictable antics of Bed Check Charlie was put out of commission with the introduction of P-38 airplanes to Henderson Field, now the air base from which American planes operated. We only endured one air raid after we arrived.

This island was quite different from New Caledonia. Lunga Point was a sandy beach that led to a flat inland area of outwash plains from the mountains. Lagoons and mangrove swamps were scattered along the shoreline, and far inland were the mountains and the rainforests. The naval base administrative offices, the galley, and mess hall where we ate were located across the road from our warehouse and offices on the beach. The whole area had been, and still was, a coconut plantation, and many of the trees had been cut down to accommodate the base.

Coconut palms were everywhere, and were systematically aligned, just like orchards of any other fruit. Our understanding was that they were either owned or controlled by Lever Brothers Soap Co., makers of Lifebuoy Soap. You could always identify new recruits, because they were so fascinated by the coconuts lying around everywhere, and the first thing they would do would be to whip out the bolo knife they always carried, and begin to chip away at the outer husk on the fruit. With enough effort they could finally produce the hairy, brown football shaped form as usually seen on your green-grocer's shelves. Punching the hull produces the milk, which is not bad tasting, but taken in large amounts is sure to bring on a case of the G. I. Trots.

The Naval Base Administration Office at Guadalcanal, in the middle of a coconut grove

After such an experience, one is not likely to tempt fate a second time, but becomes convinced that coconut is best shredded and put on a cake, but there were no cakes available. The coconuts had not been harvested for some time, and tended to accumulate as they fell off the trees. One of the hazards of living in a coconut orchard is the danger of being hit by falling fruit. It has been said facetiously that more Americans were injured at Guadalcanal by falling coconuts than by Japanese bullets. This was not true, but falling coconuts were definitely a hazard to be considered. One learned to recognize the swishing sound made as a falling coconut fell through the palm fronds, and to holler "incoming!!" and hit the ground. Another fascinating feature associated with the palms were the hundreds of brightly colored parrots that flew about in them, raucously screaming in a cacophonous frenzy.

The marines were gone by the time we came to Guadalcanal, having moved on to chase the Japanese from other islands. The CBs had finished the construction of Henderson Airfield, and the P-38s were effectively keeping Japanese plans away. Landing Force Equipment Depot was now the advanced supply base for amphibious operations that Noumea had been. Our operation had expanded to over ten times the size it had first been in Noumea.

This expansion had been necessary in order to be able to supply the advance bases that were being established. Now over a hundred men were under Commander Bean's command. He had become a full commander with scrambled eggs on his cap. All of the original ten storekeepers had been promoted to second and then to first class. A young Ensign had been added to the officer's roster before we left Noumea. He was an Ivy League product, and must have been all of nineteen. He could have been the original model for Lt. Fuzz of the Beetle Bailey comic strip fame. He must have felt out of place in our rough and ready society.

We now had an abundance of seaman assigned to us as storekeeper strikers, and a number of them soon advanced to petty officer ratings. There were also other ratings beside storekeeper assigned to us as well, particularly motor machinists and seamen in the repair department. One of the better additions to our group was a young regular Navy chief storekeeper assigned to us from the fleet. Chief Barnes had red curly hair, and had a perpetual grin on his face. He had been a professional boxer, and continued boxing

Warehouse Lunga Point: Kaler E. Bowl, Rober Erskin, Samuel Benn, James Douglas, Aldaco, D. D. Clark, Gavin Butler

after he joined the Navy. He was a very good boxer and had several bouts staged on the island while we were stationed there, all of which he won. We also made some money betting on him. He liked to smoke cigars and was a great poker player. In addition to this large work force, we had the benefit of army working parties when additional labor was needed for large outgoing shipments.

Priority items were often sent to us by air from the States and were off-loaded to us at Henderson Field. They consisted of such things as neoprene impellers for the landing craft water pumps. The distribution of these impellers were personally approved by Commander Bean, and with these impellers went his special stern lecture to the recipient concerning the disastrous effects of running the engine when the boat was not in the water. The impellers were water lubricated and would burn out if run dry for any appreciable time. Of course the person operating the boat would have to balance this possible burnout against having his boat fail to start after it was in the water. In an invasion it was important to be ready and running without delay.

We did not have airfreight coming in every day, but it became important for us to check every day because the Red Cross served free hot coffee and doughnuts to transients at Henderson Field. We were not transients, but we could pass for being them. It was also important for us to occasionally see a white woman, and the doughnuts were served to us by very pleasant young female volunteers. It was Leitz's job to drive the truck, and there would always be a scramble to see who would go with him. We reasoned that the theoretical freight might be very heavy and that extra manpower would be needed to unload it. Leitz was a good friend, and I often would be a passenger with him in the truck.

One event that broke the monotony on Lunga Point was an unexpected visit from PT skipper Billy Farr, an old friend from Carrizo Springs. He was running errands in his boat between Tulagi and Guadalcanal, and I think he was stationed in Tulagi for a short while. He was a hero to us because of his joint action in fighting the Japanese with fellow PT boat hero and president-to-be John F. Kennedy. Billy took me for a spin out in the bay in his boat, which was quite a thrill. He was later to return to the States and go into training for a Navy pilot. He completed his training just as the war ended and saw no more action in the war. His father had been a pilot in WWI, and I think this was what influenced him to go into flight training. Later that night, we had barbecue in our tent courtesy of Bernardi and liquid refreshments courtesy of Billy. It was a great reunion with an old friend.

The marines were gone when we were on Guadalcanal, but they sometimes returned for R & R. It is difficult to think of Guadalcanal as being an R & R station, but it was, compared to the hell they had been through. We got along with them fine when we met, and there are two things I remember about their visit. One was that they had souvenirs to sell, and the other was that they had sake. I did not invest in samurai swords or other weapons, or even Japanese flags. But I did trade for some invasion money, printed by the Japanese for use

Warehouse Lunga Point Crane Crew; crew quarters (tents) in background

in occupied countries. It seems that the marines had captured the Japanese paymaster.

The story was that the marine commanding officer had lined up the troops and paid each marine a portion of the captured money. I was glad to get the money for a souvenir, and I still have it. I also made my first acquaintance with sake by purchasing some from the marines. My understanding was that sake was a mild rice wine. It may have been made from rice, but it was far from being mild. This they had also captured this from the Japanese. As I have mentioned before, alcoholic beverages were restricted from naval stations, and except for occasional beer rations, which were very rare, spirits were denied the troops. Occasionally some of the cooks would brew something using canned fruits or raisins with yeast, but you would not really want to drink it. I discovered that this sake was more like brandy, and was a very potent drink, and had a kick like a government mule. I haven't had much of a taste for sake since that time.

The food we had on Guadalcanal was no better or worse than what we had been used to on Noumea. We ate at the naval base and pretty well had to eat what we were given, except for special occasions when we enjoyed some of Bernardi's largess. We had a lot of the traditional Spam, which while monotonous, wasn't really bad. We had quite a bit of meat that was mostly good, except for the mutton stew. It has been my experience that service personnel will eat just about anything that you put in front of them, but you can expect them to complain. But the mutton stew received a massive thumbsdown from the troops. We called it Royal New Zealand Goat, and refused to eat it. We could not believe that the Kiwis and Aussies liked mutton, and would even trade us beef for mutton. I think that memories of that mutton stew spoiled my appetite for anything edible that comes from a sheep.

Another traditional food we had a lot of was chipped beef on toast, which traditionally went by the more profane name of something on a shingle, or sometimes just abbreviated to SOS. Drinks were coffee, tea, or lemonade made from powder, affectionately called battery acid. All milk was powdered, and all vegetables were canned, and all eggs were powdered eggs.

I went two years without any fresh vegetables or fresh milk. These were the foods most missed. Bernardi's reefer could furnish us with occasional beef, but it couldn't provide us with vegetables or milk. Baked goods were always excellent in the Navy. And even the beans were good, but I could never get used to that old Navy tradition of having them for breakfast every Saturday morning.

One additional item added to our meals that we were not used to was our daily Atabrine tablet that was personally popped into our mouth by a pharmacist mate. This was for protection against malaria. A high percentage of the troops contracted malaria by being bitten by mosquitoes. Most of the mosquitoes were eradicated soon after the troops landed, but it was impossible to get them all, and malaria continued to be a problem.

Atabrine would not keep you from contracting malaria, but it would protect you against the disease as long as you continued to take the tablets. It had the side effect of turning your skin a yellow hue. Nobody liked taking the pills, but it was necessary. When you got back to the States and quit taking the pills, you would then know if you had malaria or not. Another fever that was prevalent was called dengue fever. Its symptoms were high fever and body aches. That I had more than once, and I did not enjoy it.

We did not often have the opportunity to come in contact with the natives. They looked just like the Kanaks on New Caledonia, very black, well built, and with black, kinky hair often bleached with lye, which produced a sort of henna nightmare mixture of black, bleached white, and red. We would occasionally see some of the men along the beach casting their nets for fish. We never saw any women on the island.

They had seashells, hand wrought knives, and primitive carved wooden war clubs to trade. I came home with two knives, three war clubs, and a bucket full of seashells. Most of these I still have. We never really saw much of the natives until we made a trip to nearby Savo Island where there was a village.

We were usually free on Sundays, and one such Sunday we were permitted to take a tank lighter with as many of our crew as wished to go. We carried a lot of blue and white flag bunting and a considerable amount of sugar courtesy of the galley. They had no use for money and were interested in bartering only. They were friendly, but shy. In time, we were able to talk to them, mostly in sign language. The kids came out soon to mingle with us, the men some time later, but it was a considerable length of time before we saw any women. Of course,

what we mostly wanted was pictures, and we were able to get some. Soup had a picture made into Christmas cards of himself alongside a dusky, busty, nubile maiden. The families lived in typical tropical grass huts. We parted friends, and came home the same afternoon.

Only once did any of our crew have an opportunity to travel inland on the island other than our trips to Henderson Field. On another Sunday, when we were on liberty and had no pressing work in progress, a number of us received permission to take our old Dodge pickup and head inland toward the mountains. The old truck did just fine on the level roads, but it was a different matter when we got off the beaten track along the coast and began to climb into the foothills. A good deal of the time was spent outside pushing rather than inside riding. We finally did penetrate into the forest, and from there on it was all climbing on foot.

I had never been in a jungle before, and I suppose that I had seen too many movies of natives hacking their way through almost impenetrable vegetation. We found ourselves walking in complete shade, and looking up at the tops of trees far above me gave me an eerie feeling. What amazed me most was the almost complete lack of ground cover. There was just too much shade, and the lack of sunlight did not permit plant growth. I could not identify the different kinds of trees, but the forests were known to contain many different kinds of hardwoods such as mahogany. The presence of sandalwood has already been mentioned. Having discovered no Japanese souvenirs, we soon got tired of walking around in the woods, and so returned to camp. What a shocking tragedy awaited us. During our absence, a small reconnaissance plane had crashed into our camp during a rainstorm.

Erskine, our machinist mate, was killed, and two of our seaman strikers so badly injured that they had to be evacuated. All this excitement, and we missed it. If we had not gone exploring, I might not be writing these memoirs. We buried Erskine in a beautiful cemetery by the local native church run by the Catholic Missionaries. I was one of the pallbearers, and it was a very sad day for all of us, having to bury one of our comrades.

Time continued on, and almost two years overseas began to take its toll on the original crew of Landing Force Equipment Depot. Bernardi grew a beard, black and curly, and of heroic proportions. With his dark skin and hooked nose, he could have passed for Moses. He had his picture taken au natural and sent some copies to his girlfriend. He was writing half dozen or so other girls, and Commander Bean thought that they all should have a copy. When he was censoring the mail, he slipped a copy to each of his girlfriends. Of course, he should not have done this, but if you could have known Bernardi, you would have said that it was poetic justice.

I first grew a mustache, and then later a Van Dyke. Still later, this progressed to a rather impressive French Empire spike mustache. I had no mustache wax, so I used cosmoline from the coating around the spare parts. I also had a parrot. I only had one more step to take, and that was to have had a gold earring. Shades of Long John Silver, some of us had been gone from home too long.

Anticipating our being rotated to the States, we were being eased out of our jobs and given lighter duties. I was promoted to Beach Master and put in charge of outgoing and incoming cargo. This was not a very taxing job if we were not preparing a major shipment to an advance base. So I spent several weeks on the beach dressed in a pith helmet and shorts and wearing cut down combat boots. Almost universally when not working in mud or muck, the combat boots were converted to low cuts for comfort. I passed a good bit of the time looking for seashells and watching the Kanaks throw their fishing nets.

Rotation Stateside

The time finally came for all the original crew to be sent home. The chiefs went first. Chief Horn was a great lover of classical music, and not only had a nice collection, but had procured by some means an old hand cranked portable Victrola. When he left, he bequeathed me the machine and some of his records. I did not keep the record player very long, as I knew that we would soon be leaving. I finally sold it to one of the strikers for fifty dollars. Unfortunately, he had a few country music records, but luckily he broke the spring in the machine, and we were spared the sound of nasal wailing. Finally the great moment arrived, and our original ten storekeepers, who were all first class except for Soup, who had made chief, climbed the gangplank, saluted the flag, and boarded the USS General Hershey, a new troopship that was used to shuttle troops back and forth across the Pacific. The ship was fast, the trip was short and uneventful, and except for sleeping in hammock-like bunks six high and crowded mess conditions, rather restful.

Along with us were many walking wounded, young men, shattered by the war, who would never be whole again. Seeing these men who had sacrificed so much seemed to bring out mixed feelings. You of course felt sorry for their plight, but you had a secret feeling of shame for being so hale and hearty, and free of any disabilities. Then, deep down inside of yourself, the secret feeling of "Gee, I'm sorry for you, but I am so glad that it isn't me."

We pulled into San Francisco and all cheered to see the Golden Gate Bridge. We disembarked to band music and a marine guard, but I had a feeling that it was all for the wounded on board, and not for us. We were quickly transported to the Treasure Island Receiving Station and began to enjoy being back in the United States. This enormous naval facility had been created from old World Fair buildings to accommodate the naval personnel transfers.

We were immediately stuffed with the best food I had ever eaten in the Navy. Hungry sailors who hadn't had fresh vegetables or milk for many months mobbed the salad bar and the milk bar. There were no restrictions concerning how much food you put on your tray, but you had better be able to eat it all. A stern looking cook watched the discards carefully, and if you threw anything out, you received a reprimand.

We were given a lecture on how to behave ourselves in San Francisco and received a 72-hour pass while our leave papers were being prepared. I went ashore with our group and immediately reserved a hotel room. We went to a restaurant and dined on fresh seafood. I soon recognized that this was not the same San Francisco I remembered from two years ago. It was not because people were hostile, because they were not. But the city, as large as it was, was saturated with servicemen.

During the course of the evening, I was sitting down by the phone booths in a hotel lobby while some of the group were making phone calls home. We had had some liquid libations, but considered ourselves to be relatively sober and causing no problems. I must have fallen asleep, because the next thing I remember is being in a room with a lot of other sailors. I suddenly sobered, and realized that I had been picked up by the shore patrol. All I could think of was my thirty-day leave going down the drain. I got up and quickly walked away. I had no money, no wallet, and no neckerchief, but I did have my hat, my pea coat, and a hotel room. I went to my hotel, turned in, and hoped for a better day tomorrow.

I ran into some of our group the next morning, bought a neckerchief, and felt respectful again. I called home and had some money sent by Western Union. I made it back to Treasure Island and was ready to go on leave. Over three years later, the Navy returned to me my wallet, my money, and my neckerchief.

The next morning I was on a train again, this time headed east. Mother and Dad were at Eagle Pass, Texas, at this time, where Dad was working as an electrician on the air base there. I had been writing several girls while I had been overseas, but I had no serious romantic entanglements with any of them.

One girl I had been dating before I went into the service had married a Border Patrolman, another had joined the WAVES, and a girl I had been writing at the Eagle Pass Airbase got married the week I got there. In two years you can become lost and forgotten. But I did enjoy my leave visiting friends and relatives, and traveled from Eagle Pass to Carrizo Springs, San Antonio, Austin, and Corpus Christi. It was too soon over, and I found myself on a train heading west to California again.

I did not enjoy the trip as much this time. I reported in at Treasure Island Naval Base to be reassigned. As I have said before, Commander Bean did his best to take care of his men. He had been very careful to attach to every one of our records a strong recommendation that we be assigned for duty to the Headquarters of the Amphibious Forces at Mechanicsburg, Pennsylvania, and explained that we were experts in the field, and had had extensive training and personal experience in the field. I had visions of meeting an apple-cheeked, blond Pennsylvania-Dutch girl and riding off into the sunset with her.

These dreams were rudely shattered when the Yeoman on duty scarcely glanced at the recommendation that that Commander Bean had so carefully worded, before tossing it into the trash basket, and tersely announcing that there were only two choices, destroyers and aircraft carriers. I was so stunned that I made no choice. Let the Navy have their way with me; so much for Commander Bean's careful plans. At least he did try.

We learned later that after we had left, he wrote out his own orders, went to Henderson Field, and flew back to San Francisco. What happened to him afterwards, I do not know. I hope that he was not court marshaled, but he could have been.

I was assigned temporarily as a night receiving petty officer to sign in sailors reporting in for duty after office hours. This was not a demanding job, but was similar to the duties of a night clerk in a hotel. There was a cot, and I could sleep as long as no one needed my services. I had the daytime off, and could go on liberty if I wished. It was not a job many people would want, because you had to work at night when all the fun was going on. During the day there was little chance of getting into trouble.

I met another first class storekeeper who also worked nights, and he suggested that we get a job as warehousemen. We applied at the National Liquor distributors, and after having been cleared by the union, we were employed. We soon discovered that warehousing consisted mostly of loading and unloading cases of booze. The work was not hard, it served to pass the time, and it paid well.

I think that this is called double dipping, but in any event, instead of spending money in nightclubs, we were putting money in the bank. I only worked a few weeks, but they were sorry to see me go, as workers were scarce during the wartime conditions. I was amazed to see the street cars loaded down, bulging with people inside, and with people outside clinging on where ever they could, like so many flies on a piece of carrion. I walked wherever I was going whenever I reasonably could.

New Orleans

I was finally given orders, not to an aircraft carrier, and not to a destroyer, as I had been informed by the intrepid yeoman, but instead assigned to the USS Hecuba, AKS-12, a supply ship that was being created by modifying a Liberty ship at the Todd Shipyards, in New Orleans, Louisiana. So once again I boarded a train and headed east, this time to New Orleans. The trip was time consuming but uneventful, but my arrival in New Orleans was not. I arrived there at 1130 on New Year's Eve.

I had seen celebrations in San Diego, Los Angeles, and San Francisco, but I was not prepared to be in New Orleans on a New Year's Eve at midnight. The street was filled with revelers swigging from bottles and toasting the New Year. The shore patrolman that I reported to said that every night was a celebration in New Orleans, but things did tend to get a bit ribald on New Year's Eve. He was finally able to drive me across the Mississippi River via the ferry to the 12th naval district Naval Base at Algiers, Louisiana. Welcome to New Orleans!

New Orleans is a fun town. You are supposed to have fun there, even with a war going on. And I did enjoy liberty there. The Vieux Carre was full of life, and I enjoyed going into the century old bars and listening to the jazz music and drinking Dixie beer with oysters on the half shell. But if liberty in New Orleans was fun, life in the receiving station was not.

The Naval Base at Gretna was headquarters for the Twelfth Naval District and was quite large. Receiving Stations, as I have mentioned before, are the pits, and this one was worse than San Diego. Or maybe it was just that the war was dragging on and things were more regimented everywhere. As far as a Receiving Station is concerned, you are not ship's company, but transients, and are just an inconvenience that is in the way.

Since they are required to feed and quarter you, they try to get all they can from you, and will keep you busy doing all the dirty jobs that must be done. Chief petty officers were excused from duty at muster, but all others were assigned to working parties, whose duties included everything from sweeping streets to loading halves of frozen beef, both of which I did. While doing the latter I got beaned by a careless sailor with a meat hook. I was dazed and bleeding like a stuck pig. The person in charge of the working party reluctantly released me to go to sickbay. I walked in just at noon and was told by the pharmacist mate to come back after lunch as he slammed the admission door in my face. I could have gone someplace and washed off the blood, but I was just as hard headed as the pharmacist mate had been rude, so I just sat down and waited for an hour, dried blood and all. As the door opened, I moved in. The doctor took one look at me and hit the ceiling. I told my story and gloated while the Lt. Commander chewed out a suddenly very contrite pharmacist mate.

Now I don't mind working, and I had turned in some very long hours in the Navy, but this place was despicable. I had lost my glasses and wished to get some more made. I was examined by a pharmacist mate (not the same one of meat hook fame), who informed me that I didn't need glasses. I had been wearing them since I was eighteen. I finally demanded to see an officer, and finally talked to a Lt. Commander (no, not the same one either), who examined me and said that I could have glasses made, but I would have to go to New Orleans to get them. Hard lines! This meant that I could escape the clutches of the working parties during those times.

The reason for all this nonsense was that our ship was being refitted as a supply ship, and no officers had yet been assigned. We were in limbo until an officer could be responsible for us. In the meantime, the receiving ship was stuck with us and we were stuck with them, and they were determined to get as much as possible out of us. We were even required to obtain a walking chit from our barrack petty officer to walk down the street or go to the ship's store or the post office. Any suspicious person would be stopped by the MPs and made to show their walking chit.

To escape this insanity, I got myself assigned temporarily to the store-keeper who was the admission clerk at the Navy prison located on the base. He was a second-class storekeeper whose duty it was to log in and log out the prisoners. He was also in charge of all the personal belongings of the pris-oners while they were incarcerated. I outranked him, but that didn't matter. He felt sorry for me, and while he didn't have a lot for me to do, he created enough clerical work to keep me busy and out of trouble.

He was a cheerful little gnome of a man, somewhat older than most of the sailors. And it seemed to make him sad to see so many of the men in prison. Again, most of them were there because they were either AWOL or homosexual. He seemed shocked, as was I, that so many of them were accused of being homosexual. Anyway, he seemed to enjoy my company, and while I was only there for a few days, I did appreciate his pulling me from the quagmire of the receiving station.

The first person I met who was to be a new shipmate was a first class gunner's mate named Clements. He was regular Navy, and had been in the service since he was seventeen. He was a Texan also, and came from Uvalde. We found we had some acquaintances in common. We became good friends, and between the two of us, we managed to rent an apartment in New Orleans so that we could cut one more tie with the receiving station, so that we did not have to sleep at the base every night. We kept it, and both used it and even lent it out until his girlfriend moved from Uvalde and came to New Orleans to be with him.

Clements

In the meantime other members of the crew began to show up, and we became a cohesive unit. In addition to Clements and myself, there were two officers, a chief, and several other storekeepers. We were given various assignments. My job was mostly clerical work, and I spent most of my time in the office, with occasional trips to the ship that was tied up to the dock nearby.

The ship was awash with workers hammering, riveting, and painting, and all the while sparks were flying everywhere from welders patching pieces of metal together. This was to be our home, and we worked and watched as she was converted from a liberty ship to a supply ship for the US Navy, the AKS-12, USS Hecuba. I was amazed at the number of women welders working on the ship. They must have done a good job, for as time was to prove, she was able to plow through some very stormy seas.

Even although we were assigned to the ship, we still slept in the barracks when we had to and ate our meals at the mess hall. Occasionally when I was in the barracks, which was not too often, I would read the notices on the bulletin board. One day I was astounded to read the following notice. "Wanted, personnel to study as storekeepers in Landing Craft Depot, Mechanicsburg, Pennsylvania. Any rate may apply." I could not believe my eyes! And then I appreciated the irony of that unknowing, uncaring rude yeoman callously tossing Commander Bean's carefully worded instructions into the wastebasket, and in a bored voice saying "aircraft carrier or destroyer." I understood that the problem was that the war had been so demanding, and military institutions had grown so rapidly, that in the government, the left hand no longer knew what the right hand was doing. I could have volunteered for this duty, but I said, "The hell with it. I will stay with the USS Hecuba," and I think I made the better choice.

Ouida Mae

It was at this time that I first met my wife-to-be. Our first meeting did not have a very auspicious beginning. As the incipient crew of the Hecuba came together, they were assigned an office in a creaky old building near the docks along the Mississippi River. While sitting at a desk in the office, a newspaper was slipped under the door from the next office. Several of the crew had commented on the good-looking red head that worked next door. I thought "how nice, the young lady next door is giving me a paper to read." I removed it and began to read. Another newspaper was slipped under the door, and again I thought "How very nice. Here comes the rest of the paper." About that time an irate redhead burst into the room and demanded to know who was pulling the paper from under the door. It seems that the paper had been put there to block out the glare from the sun that was shining in her eyes.

Actually she didn't seem to care whether we sailors had a paper to read or not. And that was my rather abrupt introduction to Miss Ouida Mae Hinyub. In spite of this rather bizarre introduction, we did soon go out on a date. I was impressed with her kindness and consideration while dealing with people, and especially her willingness in trying to be helpful. It seemed to me that she was forever going out of her way to assist some bewildered sailor to find a place for his wife, or visiting relatives to stay, or to help with placing long distance calls, or some  other favor a native of New Orleans could do much more easily than a seventeen year old recruit.

Our first date was not momen-
tous. We went roller-skating, and I
am sure that I did not impress her,
certainly not with my skating. But
we did continue dating, though we
never went roller-skating again. We
did a lot of other fun things. There
were a lot of things you could do in
New Orleans, even during the war.
We saw movies, went to plays, and
even went to wrestling matches. In
a very short time, we were going
out together every time we could.
She wanted me to go to Slidell to
visit her folks. This is always a scary

thing to do. The Southern Railway station was in downtown New Orleans.
It was a beautiful building made of marble, and unfortunately, it has since
been torn down. We could take the train and be in Slidell in less than an hour.
I got a room at the hotel across from the train station, and we walked to her
house that was only a block away.

Her folks were friendly enough, but it did give me a funny feeling when
her father, known by everyone as Mr. Shorty, brought out a new shotgun to
show us. It would have made me feel a lot funnier if I had known that Mr.
Shorty did not go hunting, and did not care anything about guns. But in any
event, they were very nice to me, and we had a pleasant weekend.

By this time we had a sort of unspoken agreement that we would be
together whenever we could. I had been buried in the South Pacific for two
years without any possibility of female companionship, and since then had
not been in one place long enough to really come in contact with the same.
Now I had found someone whom I enjoyed being with, and, in fact, we
seemed to enjoy each other's company. It was a comfortable relationship for
both of us.

The USS Hecuba

Meanwhile, the USS Hecuba was taking shape. She was rather quickly changing from an ordinary Liberty ship to a US Navy supply ship. As a Navy ship in time of war, she was armed, but only marginally so. She had a three-inch gun forward and a five-inch aft and batteries of 20 mm anti-aircraft guns amidships. She was not exactly bristling with armament, but she carried a little bit of a sting. Principally she was designed as a shopping center for ships of the Pacific Fleet.

As the Hecuba was a supply ship, she carried an unusually large supply of storekeepers. I can remember only the names of those I was closely associated with. Beginning with the officers, here is a thumbnail sketch of the crew of the USS Hecuba.

Our Captain was Commander Castle. He was a former tugboat captain and was one of the Castles of the consortium of Castle and Cook of Hawaii, a coalition that at that time owned about half of the state. He was a dark-haired, beetle-browed hulk of a man, standing at least 6 foot 4 inches tall. He was a fair man, and well liked by the crew. His First Officer was Lieutenant Commander Benthusen, a hard-bitten old mustang who had been in the Navy all his adult life. A mustang is an enlisted man that has come up through the enlisted ranks and has been commissioned as an officer. They usually stand apart because they are not as well educated as the other officers who graduated from Annapolis.

My boss was the Supply Officer, Lieutenant Byers. He was a pudgy-faced, stocky man who spent most of his time in the office and left the running of the storerooms to the first class and chief Petty Officers. There was a Warrant Officer and a Chief in the office, but I do not remember their names. The only other ship's officer I remember was the Engineering Officer. I remember him because he was a New Mexico native, and his family owned half the state. We had the unusual distinction of having two millionaires on board — the Captain and the Engineering Officer.

Most of the storekeepers on board came into the Navy under the V-6 program. That is, we had volunteered for the duration of the war and six months. Certainly very few harbored the notion of staying in the Navy after the end of the war. One exception was Tony, one of the two Chief Storekeepers aboard the ship. He was Italian, had a very slight build, did not have a very good education, and mostly seemed to wander around the deck of the ship. I don't remember his last name.

As I have remarked before, the Hecuba, being a supply ship, abounded with storekeepers and seaman striking for storekeeper. I remember a few of their names, but most are a part of my memory only as faces, and when I look at a picture of S Company, as we were then known, not only are there names that I cannot recall, but there are also faces that are not familiar to me. Here is a thumbnail sketch of the few shipmates that I can recall:

- Cook, who we called Cookie for no reason I can remember, was a second-class storekeeper who worked in the office. He was one of the early birds whom I met at our office on the dock.

- Hudson was a first class storekeeper from Pasadena, California. He was sturdily built with rugged facial features, and had black hair starting to turn prematurely gray. He was good humored, hard working, and eager to get the war over so that he could return to California and his wife. He and I were to go into partnership on some dubious business aboard ship.

- Kenneth Holliday was a second-class storekeeper who came from Somerset, Iowa, and whose father owned a candy store. We were always delighted when he got a care package from home. My most vivid remembrance of him is the time he came in too close a contact with a cesspool on his way back to the ship from a liberty in New Orleans, and came unsteadily up the gangplank smelling not exactly like a rose. He swore he was sober.

- Rustuccio was a short, dark-skinned Italian from Boston. He had worked as a shoemaker and was always giving us a lecture on the best kind of shoes to buy. We were always making fun of him because of his Boston accent, which bothered him not at all. His wife came to visit him in New Orleans before the ship left. She was a roly-poly little lady almost as short as Rustuccio, and just as jolly.

- Rourk was a pudgy third class storekeeper who came from Michigan and had been in the furniture business. His advice to me was, "Never pay full price when you buy furniture. There is always someone who can get it for you wholesale." Sadly I do not remember the names of the many other storekeepers aboard the ship.

Time began to pass swiftly as spring began to turn to summer. The Hecuba was rapidly being converted to a supply ship from a Liberty ship. Compartments and bins had been added, she got a new paint job, and she was degaussed. Finally the crew was moved aboard. It was now the skipper's turn to show off. He took her out into the Mississippi under her own power, and being an ex–tugboat commander, he insisted on turning her around in the river while two tugboats stood by watching him nervously. We shifted our mooring from Gretna to Westwego down river.

Next came the commissioning of the ship and our commissioning party, and now we were officially the USS Hecuba, AKS-12, and we were ready to go to sea. The skipper had said to the crew that there would be no June brides, and he was right. We left on our shakedown cruise of May 31 after a short farewell to those left behind. However, later we found out that Chief Tony had jumped the gun and married a Cajun girl. The prediction was that they would be separated before the Hecuba returned to the States.

It was interesting sailing down the Mississippi. The delta is not heavily populated, but we did pass a few small towns. We saw a number of nutria, a large rodent imported from South America that were well adapted to the environment of the delta and thrived there. We also began to be accompanied by an escort of dolphins, the occurrence of which is considered by sailors to be a sign of good luck. The river splits into a number of tributaries, so that the process of getting from the river to the ocean is no easy task. So complex a matter is this that a pilot is required to conduct the ship through the complexities of the shifting pattern of this mighty river.

Our shakedown cruise was a short one, as we sailed only as far as Galveston, Texas. There we stayed several days so that any discrepancies that had occurred during the trip could be corrected. As these chores required some time, those of the crew who lived nearby were granted 72-hour leave. Clements and I both took advantage of this serendipity and started hitchhiking. Sailors had no problem getting rides from people, but the problem was that there was very little automobile traffic during the war. We finally got a train that took us to San Antonio, and there we split up, he going to Uvalde, and I to Eagle Pass. It was one last fling before going back to war.

When I arrived back at the ship at Galveston, I found two important letters waiting for me. One was from Soup Bole telling me that he had been assigned to the USS Cybele, AKS-10. The other one was a sad one telling me that John Mullins, then Captain Mullins, had been killed while making a parachute jump in the invasion of the Philippines. We left Galveston the next day and began our trek back to the war in the Pacific. The most interesting event of this part of the trip was our passage through the Panama Canal. It was our most fervent wish that there would be a bottleneck for ships going through the canal and that we would be delayed enough to have opportunities for liberty at Colon or Panama City.

Alas, it was not to be. We were not even slowed down going through the canal, but moved swiftly through the locks. I was fascinated by the way huge ships could be raised or lowered by pumping or draining water in or out of the locks. We soon cleared the canal and found ourselves in the Pacific. The deep blue, almost purple color of the water in the Pacific Ocean always fascinated me, as did the phosphorescent trace of the ship's wake by night. I had been in the Navy for over two years, yet as a sailor I was a complete fraud. Except for going and coming to the Pacific, I had had no experience as a real sailor. Now, for the first time, I was on a ship as an integral part of the ship, not just as a passenger. I was part of the ship's company of the USS Hecuba, AKS-12.

As anyone who travels on a ship at sea soon discovers, life on board a ship is quite different from life on land. It takes time to get used to a heaving deck whose center of gravity is always changing as you walk upon it. It also affects ones balance upon returning to tread on land, and the rolling walk that a sailors just off a ship have is not always due to the unwise use of strong drink, but to a changed relationship between your feet and the ground. Hence the old sea dog's expression "I have to get my sea legs back" and visa versa. Many people are affected by mal de mer, but it never bothered me, even in violent storms.

The closest I ever came to becoming sea sick was when I was trying to recover from a night on the town and was resting on a bunch of life jackets in a tank lighter tied up to a dock. Small craft passing by created a wake, and the rocking motion made me feel queasy, so that I had to reluctantly give up my resting place and go back to work or I might have become sea sick.

Back to the Pacific

The trip to Hawaii, our first port of call, was uneventful. We were traveling alone, not in convoy, and we were sailing a wartime zigzag pattern. We went a little bit out of our way so that we could pass by Easter Island, but of course we could not stop. Join the Navy and see the world — through a porthole. We arrived at Honolulu and enjoyed our first liberty in Hawaii.

This was Captain Castle's home, so it was a real homecoming for him. He was a good captain who genuinely seemed to care about the welfare of his crew, and he gave us a lecture over the loud speaker about the places to go and not go in the city.

I was able to take a trip to the other side of the island across the Pali, as the pass across the mountains is called, and see the beautiful beaches on the other side. Waikiki beach is not much of a beach by comparison. In fact, they have to haul sand into Waikiki to have a beach at all, as the currents tend to carry the sand away from the land.

I also visited the pineapple plantations, drank my fill of free pineapple juice, and rode the midget trains of the Pineapple Line that carried people and produce to and from Honolulu. The people were friendly, but we found it to be just as it had been in San Diego — that the sheer number of sailors inundated Honolulu.

The Pali — 1945

We were not long in Hawaii, and soon found ourselves engaged in the performance of our duties, which was to furnish the ships of the fleet with the supplies that they needed. Other than food, medical supplies, and ammunition, we were the country store of our part of the Pacific. We carried cordage, electrical supplies, tools, clothing, and ship store stock, which included everything from toothpaste to candy bars, cigarettes, and beer.

A more accurate explanation of our duties would be to compare us to the old-fashioned "drummer" or traveling salesman that carried his goods with him as he made the rounds of his country customers. Our pattern of travel was from Hawaii to Ulithi, an atoll in the Caroline Group, and next door to Bikini, which was to gain fame as the site of an atomic bomb test.

From there, we went to Eniwetok, one of the Marshall Group of islands, and thence back to Hawaii to be restocked. If this sounds familiar, you may be remembering the World War II novel and movie "Mr. Roberts," concerning a similar situation in which a ship made repeated trips to islands which they called Boredom, Tedium, and Apathy. Just as they sailed from Tedium to Boredom to Apathy, we sailed from Hawaii to Ulithi and Eniwetok, and then back to Hawaii.

This continued for a number of months, and although we were busy, it was boring. The crew found different ways to pass the time. One of the radio operators liked to fish, and he spent his spare time casting a line off of the fantail. His best catch was a twelve-pound Pompano. The cook prepared it, and some lucky ones got a bite or two of it. My friend Clements, the gunner's mate, spent time cleaning the guns in the armory, and we sometimes had target practice with rifles, BARs, and Thompson machine guns.

My friend Hudson and I helped prevent boredom and made a few dollars for ourselves in a rather nefarious manner. We had pooled our money in New Orleans and purchased a number of punchboards and a miniature slot machine. We reasoned that we were providing entertainment, and so were entitled to a profit, which we did make. The punchboards always would make money when they sold out. The slot machine could be adjusted to give the customer a break, or set so that he must lose.

The Master at Arms raised hell when he found punchboard slips littering the deck. The Supply Officer, Lieutenant Byers, heard about the slot machine and came down into the hold to see it. He spun it one time, shook his head, and left. I guess he thought it was good entertainment also. After that, we were a little more circumspect with our operations. We eventually sold the remainder of our punchboards and the slot machine for a nice profit in the Philippines. Neither Hudson nor I felt any remorse about our gambling devices. It is true we made a little money on them, but we reasoned that we were entitled to it, first because we had the initiative to think of them, and secondly we felt they had served their purpose as entertainment for the troops.

Another paradox that existed on board the Hecuba was that we carried hundreds of cases of beer aboard, but were not permitted to drink any aboard the ship. To paraphrase Coleridge, "Beer, beer everywhere, and all the throats did shrink, beer, beer everywhere, nor any drop to drink." In order for us to drink beer, it was necessary to go ashore as a liberty party. I tried it once in Ulithi. It is not much fun to drink warm beer on a pile of sand under a coconut tree with a bunch of drunken sailors. However, Yankee ingenuity will find a way. We were not allowed to buy beer ourselves, but proper authority could make purchases for their ships. We simply added beer purchases to a customers chit, gave him the money to pay for the beer, put the purchased beer in one of a thousand random hiding places aboard the ship, and everyone was happy. As long as we were circumspect and did not abuse the privilege, the system worked very well. Whisky was strictly forbidden aboard ship. I knew this and very casually brought aboard a case of Ancient Age bourbon fifths that Mr. Shorty had bought for me by bringing it with the rest of my gear right up the gangplank past the Officer of the Deck. Thus my friends and I could celebrate birthdays, anniversaries, and bad hair days.

Final Days of the War

The war was coming to an end. The Battle of Leyte Gulf drove the Japanese back, and MacArthur retook the Philippines. We were at sea when the war with Japan came to an end, and the captain came on the ship's intercom with the news. An appreciable amount of the Ancient Age disappeared that night. It was on this voyage that we ran into a typhoon. This was my second experience with this type of storm, and I was beginning to build up respect for them and what they could do. I was much more concerned about it than I had been with the storm on the Sommelsdijk. Winds were in excess of 90 knots. Waves pounding the side of the ship broke all the mirrors fastened to the bulkhead in the enlisted men's head, and I was standing in the supply office when a particularly rough series of rolls of the ship tossed me around like dice shaken in a cup. The destruction from this same type of storm was so disastrous on Okinawa at a later date that we were diverted there to supply clothing and other necessities. This caused us to remain longer in the Pacific than we would have otherwise and delayed our return to the States.

It might be well at this time to give a little thought to weather forecasting and the meteorological advancements that were made during WWII. American four engine bombers flying from advance bases in the Pacific to bomb Japan often encountered high speed winds that forced them to abort their flights. The existence of such high velocity winds had not been suspected before. These winds are tubular in shape, faster in their core than on the outside, and sinuous in nature, changing position constantly. Their position and velocity were found to have a profound effect on the weather on the surface of the ground. Twisting winds of high velocity are called typhoons in the Pacific and hurricanes in the Atlantic.

They seem to be more formidable in the Pacific, possibly because of the enormous size of the ocean. Storms are able to continue for almost unlimited distances while meeting almost no obstructions in the form of land. By either name they are terrible agents of destruction. On December 17, 1943, the Third Fleet under Admiral Halsey encountered bad weather while making air strikes against the Philippines. This bad weather developed into the granddaddy of all typhoons, which severely battered the fleet. Three destroyers were lost, seven other ships were damaged, and almost eight hundred men lost their lives. This was the greatest setback of the Navy since the Battle of Savo Island, and the Japanese never fired a shot.

The following description of this monstrous typhoon is taken directly from Hanson W. Baldwin's writings from *The United States Navy in World War II*:

> The ships, big and little, are racked and strained, punished and pummeled. The men are dazed; all hands are in life jackets; none stand topside in exposed positions; muscles are sore, and bodies are bruised from clinging to stanchions, pounding against bulkheads; a miserable many retch from seasickness, but for hundreds terror calms the queasiness of the stomach. The violent rolls and the terrible mountains of water — seventy feet from cross to crest — are frightening, even to the experienced; some are plain scared, but most have confidence in the stoutness of their vessels. The voice of the storm drowns out all other voices. The wind has a thousand notes — the bass of growling menace, the soprano of stays so tightly strained they hum like bowstrings. The tops of the wave crests are flattened off by the wind and hurled straight before its violence. Rain and spindrift mix in a horizontal sheet of water, and one cannot tell where ocean stops and sky begins. And over all is the cacophony of the ships — the creaking of the bulkheads, the working of the stanchions, the play of the rivets, the hum of the blowers, the slide and tear and roar of chairs, and books adrift, of wreckage slipping from bulkhead to bulkhead.

We survived our typhoon to reach Pearl Harbor to be resupplied. With the war over, we abandoned our Ulithi-Eniwetok schedule, and headed for the Philippines to supply the Third Fleet. We were hoping to berth in Manila, but it was not to be, and instead we were assigned to Tacloban, a much smaller city than Manila. We were tied up to the dock and were free to go ashore, but Tacloban was not a good liberty town. The war was just over, and the people of the Philippines were in miserable condition and striving to overcome the devastation caused by the Japanese invasion. There were people living near the ship, and we were able to go ashore and visit with them. They were friendly enough, but they were desperately poor and struggling to survive. We spent several weeks in the Philippines. From there we were sent to Okinawa. This island had suffered a terrible, devastating storm. Another typhoon had struck, but this time most of the damage was to buildings and habitations on land.

57

Okinawa

This would be the closest we would come to the Islands of Japan. Chief Kaler (Soup) Bole was destined to sail into Tokyo Bay on the Cybele, AKS-10, directly behind the USS Missouri, and to witness the signing of the peace treaty. They later traveled to main land China, and there he purchased for me numerous souvenirs, including a carved sandalwood box and an opium pipe. But the destiny of the USS Hecuba, AKS-12, was to languish in the harbor at Okinawa. We weren't even privileged to tie up at a dock, but were anchored out in the bay. I was able to go ashore for one day while there, and see for myself first hand the destruction rained down on this unfortunate island. What the Americans had not blown up, the typhoon had tried to blow away. There was a water taxi that made regular runs between the ships and shore, and he deposited me on the docks. From there it was easy to thumb a ride from the constant traffic of trucks and jeeps. Everywhere there was evidence of the horrendous bombardment this island had undergone. This was most evident in the city of Naha, which was the largest city and capitol of the island. It was a silent city of utter destruction. There was no activity there, and no people at all in the city except the Americans troops. What was left of the civilian population had been herded into prisoner of war camps behind barbed wire and guarded by MPs. The residential sections had been reduced to piles of rubble that were everywhere covered with fragments of tile that apparently had been the roofs.

As I approached the nearby seashore, I saw evidence of the intensity of the bombardment administered from invasion warships. The ground in places was paved with steel fragments from the exploding shells. A grim sight was crypts built into the side of the cliffs that had been blown apart by the naval bombardment, littering the surrounding area with human bones. I have spoken to a number of servicemen who had been stationed in Okinawa in recent times, and they speak of Naha as a city bustling with activity and having a population of thousands. This is a far cry from the desolation I witnessed that day. I hiked and hitched my way back to the other side of the island and the relative comfort of the Hecuba. The one high spot of the trip had

Shinto shrine after bombardment

been the finding of a tomato plant in an abandoned garden filled with ripe tomatoes.

We were only in Okinawa for a few weeks. As I have mentioned before, due to limited dock facilities, most ships were anchored out in the harbor. There were many ships of all kinds, and they were assigned specific locations in a grid pattern like automobiles in a parking lot. For some reason, we were ordered to change locations. This required us to up anchor and get the ship under way. Special assignments associated with moving and operating the ship are the responsibility of the bosun on duty and are handled by the appropriate sea details. The special assignments concerning raising and lowering the anchor are handled by just such a special sea detail, and it is trained to be proficient in this job. Raising an anchor which weighs many tons and which has links that weigh over two hundred pounds each is not a job for amateurs. The special anchor detail had been called and they had raised the anchor and we were under way moving slowly to our new location, alert to be ready to set the anchor when our new mooring location was reached.

Now releasing the anchor on a ship the size of the Hecuba is a delicate job because of the tremendous weight of the anchor and chains as mentioned before. A predetermined number of links had been selected to be released. The releasing mechanism for the anchor is a special device that requires a sharp blow by a small hammer to activate it. Once set in motion, it is impossible to stop the operation until the preset number of links have been run out. This sharp blow is delivered by a seaman who has his eyes riveted on this target, and his ears attuned to hear the bosun say the magic words, "Let go the anchor." The other members of the sea detail were standing by to perform any duty the bosun ordered. They were mostly young kids, and like most young kids, they were full of energy and tended to be inattentive. Two of them were clowning around and playing grab ass when one of them yelled, "Let go." What do you think happened? You guessed it. That poor seaman with his ears attuned to hear those magic words "Let go the anchor" did just that, and we had the embarrassing situation of having dropped the anchor while we were still under way. I thought that the bosun was going to have a heart attack, and the captain was shouting and pulling out all his hair. I left the scene. I reasoned that anyone who was in the area of this incident would be in trouble. I would not be surprised to hear that these seamen are still chipping paint somewhere after all these years.

We had one other interesting event that took place when we were anchored in the bay at Okinawa. A barge nearby was being pushed by two tugs. There was a strong outgoing tide surging, and the tugs were struggling with their chore. I was standing on the deck watching and suddenly realized that the barge was getting perilously close to the Hecuba. When I saw a sailor on the tug grab an ax and start hacking away at the line attached to the

Rustuccio, Holliday, unknown, unknown, Yeats; Cookie, unknown, Hudson

barge, I knew that he was cutting loose from it to avoid being caught in the middle, and I knew we were in for a collision.

I remember the incident appeared to take place in slow motion. These two large objects were drawing closer and closer together until they collided. There was no horrendous crash, but more of shuddering thud. They hung together a few seconds as if embracing, and then the barge rebounded and slowly moved away with the tugs in hot pursuit, like parents chasing a recalcitrant offspring.

I think that the Captain would wish that he had been in Okinawa and faced the awful wrath of the recent kamikaze air attacks rather than to have had this ignominy befall him. It is considered to be commendable to suffer a heroic sacrifice for your country, but it is a far worse fate to suffer being the butt of wardroom jibes about your ship being damaged by a runaway garbage scow. The only damage to the Hecuba besides that to her pride was a gotch in her bow that the barge left as a souvenir of the kiss they enjoyed.

Our duties over in Okinawa, we set sail for Hawaii. Now the crew spent much of their time considering how soon they would be eligible for discharge from the Navy. Bear in mind that most of the crew of the Hecuba as well as the rest of the Navy were V-6 volunteers or draftees and not regular Navy. Now that the war was over, all the armed services were faced with the inevitable fact that they were going to lose most of their men. These services had grown from very small numbers before the war to more than 16 Million.

Going Home

Now most of them were clamoring for release. The next year would witness the voluntary destruction of the mightiest military force that ever existed. There was a scramble by all the V-6 volunteers and the draftees to be released. The release of so many men is a very short time would leave the Navy in a very precarious position. They would be hard pressed lot maintain crews to keep the fleet afloat.

During the time of war, the Navy carried nearly twice as many men aboard ship as was necessary for their operation. This, coupled with the fact that many of their warships would soon be placed in mothballs, enabled them to maintain the fleet. Some of this mothballed fleet were called back in action, but many a proud fighting ship was scrapped forever. Some specialty ships were converted back to private use as cargo ships. Such was the fate of the Hecuba. While reading the shipping news in the newspaper one day, I saw the Hecuba's name. She was being used as a cargo ship, plying her trade between The US and South America.

The wholesale destruction of much of the fleet was necessary, but saddening. The Navy's method of discharging its men was based on a point system. The number of points a man accumulated was determined by several factors. Points were given for the number of months of service, by the number of these months that were spent overseas, and by his marital status. I thought that my nearly four years of service coupled with the fact that over thirty months were oversea duty would result in an early release. Wrong. I was single, and points were heavily weight for married men. I can understand the government's reasoning. Married men received an allotment for their family, and it was more advantageous to discharge the married men and stop the allotments than it was to discharge the single men who did not receive this allotment — not at all fair, but certainly expedient.

We arrived in Pearl Harbor and continued moving supplies as needed. While we were there, we said goodbye to Captain Castle. Hawaii was his home, and he was discharged there. Farewell to an excellent Captain. Our First Officer, Commander Benthusen, now became the Captain of the Hecuba. After several weeks, we said goodbye to Hawaii and set sail for San Francisco. For some unknown reason, we took the northern circle route, and because of this northerly position, we encountered weather much colder than that we had been used to in the Pacific

About half way to San Francisco, we encountered heavy weather, and I found myself face to face with my third typhoon. I often counsel myself that I should be very careful in the things I do, because I used up a preponderance of my allotted luck surviving typhoons in the Pacific. This was to be the worst storm of the three. And this time we did not have the naval expertise of Captain Castle, who was probably enjoying a martini sitting by his swimming pool while we were desperately trying to stay afloat. One typhoon is very much like another, except the intensity can vary widely. This one seemed to me to be the mother of all storms. Individual little vignettes come to mind when I think back on that storm. The storekeepers were responsible for seeing that the cargo in the hold was stable. On one of my inspection tours, I found that several large spools of electric cable were working loose and would require that a work crew be sent down in the hold to secure it. The rolls were large enough to damage the bulkhead if left unattended.

While I was in the process of reporting to the bridge on my watch, an enormous wave broke over the bridge. It knocked down the poor helmsman who was trying desperately to cling to the wheel, the seaman standing behind him whose job was to prevent just this sort of thing from happening, Captain Benthusen, who was acting as Officer of the Deck, and myself. The wheel was spinning free, and during the melee, everyone was struggling to get back on his feet. The Captain was shouting, "Grab the helm," and the ship was pitching wildly. Someone finally did grab the wheel, and the poor battered helmsman was propped up and again began to fight the power of the storm.

I reported to the Captain and left as soon as possible, glad to escape that particularly scary wrath of the sea. Old salts like to talk about hundred foot waves that they have seen, but they are very rare. The consensus of the crew who were qualified to know was that the waves we were seeing were within that range and that they were breaking over the bridge.

During the next day, we sailed into calmer water and were drenched by a down pouring of rain. In a short time, blue skies and bright sunshine followed the rain. I was on deck admiring the sudden good weather and congratulating myself on how lucky we had been to come through such a harrowing experience. An old Chief joined me at the rail, and when I commented on how fortunate we were to have come through such a blow, he said, "Ah laddie, its only half over. We are in the eye of the storm. It is only whirling around us, and now we have to go through the other side." It seemed unbelievable to me that we could come through such a storm into a dead calm and then be cruelly thrust back into the maelstrom again, but we were. Thankfully, it was not as severe as our first encounter, and we grimly hung on and managed to survive and move into calmer seas.

After the storm was over I noticed that our flag, which had been flying all through our travail, was down to the stars in the field of blue. We realized how lucky we were when we heard that a liberty ship of our tonnage went down with all hands in the same storm. Our navigation officer said that the atmospheric pressure at the height of the storm was the lowest he had ever seen during his many years at sea. The prediction had been made by our officers that a list of 37 degrees would sink the Hecuba. We registered 38.

Sunny skies accompanied us the rest of the cruise to San Francisco. We dropped anchor in San Francisco Bay on December 21, 1945, and those of us who were eligible were immediately sent to the Receiving Station to be discharged. All the enlisted men had been given promotions in rank except for the First Class. We could not be promoted because such a promotion required a 500 dollar payment to cover the new type clothing required for Chiefs. Not fair, but expedient. I was told that I would be promoted if I promised to stay in the Navy, but I declined.

We were quickly processed at the Naval Base, and I will say that the yeomen did yeoman duty in discharging us as quickly as possible. We were released on the 23rd of December. One of the men being released at the same time as I had purchased a surplus truck, and a number of us heading east went along with him. By sharing the driving, we were able to travel without stopping and made good time across the country. They kicked me out in Albuquerque, and I spent Christmas Day riding a bus to Artesia, New Mexico. I arrived there at midnight. Merry Christmas!!

Epilogue

In retrospect it is interesting to look back and see the changes that have taken place since World War II in New Caledonia and Guadalcanal. There was a massive pull out of troops from Noumea at the end of the war until none remained. The conflict between the French and the Kanaks peaked in 1980 when the Kanaks revolted, and seeking independence, seized towns and torched the homes of white settlers. French troops were flown in and the rebellion was put down. Peace returned to the island, and it is no longer dangerous to travel about. Nickel mining is still what makes the economy run. Prices are high, as most goods must be imported. Still, many French teachers, technicians, and bureaucrats come to invasion. After the end of World War II, people migrated to occupy the buildings and construction left behind by the US Military. They congregated around Lunga Point, where Landing Force Equipment Depot was located on Noumea, because of the higher salaries they can earn. Japanese tourists rush to expose their film on the topless beaches that abound. New Caledonia is unique in that it contains

Sunken Liberty Ship memorial at Ebeye, Marshall Islands

native plants not found anywhere else in the world. It is considered to be a botanist's paradise. Guadalcanal never contained a large population. The nearest thing to a population center was on Tulagi, and that was largely destroyed by the Japanese. There is some tourist traffic in the area today, and the road system built by the CBs is used, as is Henderson Field, which still functions as an airport.

Finally, what is the status of the 16 million service men that participated in World War II? In the year 2000, the age would largely range from the low seventies up, and they are vanishing at the rate of 1000 per day. I only hope I may do as well as my great-great-Uncle Williams who, as a Civil War veteran who fought for the Confederacy, was reported to have attained the remarkable age of 118!

Appendix A: History of the MS Sommelsdijk

The MS *Sommelsdijk*[1] was built in September 1939 by the Danish shipyard Odense Staalskibsværft in Odense, Denmark. Originally meant for the Holland-Amerika Lijn (Holland America Line) route from Rotterdam to the Dutch East Indies, she along with her sister ship *Sloterdijk* were moved to the New York to Java route as the war flared in Europe. She was in New York when Germany invaded the Netherlands in May 1940, at which point the Allies took command of her.

She was in service for a while as a freighter, but in 1942 she underwent changes to turn her into a troop transport for use in the Pacific. In May 1943, she took off from San Francisco to the Pacific islands of Fiji, Noumea, and Espiritu Santo. She made three other overseas voyages in 1943, including to Australia, Hawaii, and the Russell Islands.

In 1944, she made four trips across the Pacific, with stops in Noumea, Samoa, Eniwetok, and Papua New Guinea. On December 25, while stationed at Leyte Gulf, she was hit by a Japanese aerial torpedo in the number one lower hold which created a 20' by 30' hole in her side and caused six deaths. The hold was immediately set on fire, and for a time it appeared that the ship might be lost. The 1300 CBs on board were evacuated to the nearby HMAS *Gascoyne* and USS *Buttonwood*. Eventually, after pumping water into the affected hold, the fire was extinguished, and she was repaired on-site. She later received more permanent repairs in New York after arriving on June 30, 1945.

After the war, she was used as transport between the East Coast and Europe, still in service to the US Navy. In January 1946, she was released to her original owners, the Holland America Line, and after additional restoration, returned to commercial service in 1947.

---

[1] Most sources list the name as *Sommelsdijk* until the spelling is changed after the war, but images purportedly from 1939 (see next page) show the name as *Sommelsdyk*.

The MS *Sommelsdyk* in 1939

She was later renamed *Sommelsdyk* and continued voyages worldwide for the next twenty years. Finally, she was again renamed to *Somme* and sold to a Spanish shipbreaker to be scrapped in Burriana, Spain, on June 11, 1965.

Pacific voyages from San Francisco:

- **May 1943** Lautoka (Fiji), Noumea, Espiritu Santo

- **July 1943** Brisbane, Auckland

- **1943** Honolulu

- **November 1943** Espiritu Santo, Russell Islands, Milne Bay

- **January 1944** Noumea, Efate, Tutuila (Samoa)

- **1944** Milne Bay, Buna, Langemak, Lae

- **1944** Samoa, Suva, Lautoka, Milne Bay

- **1944** via Honolulu to Eniwetok, Saipan

- **November 1944** Milne Bay, Hollandia, Leyte (returned to New York in May 1945)

Appendix B: Wikipedia on the USS Hecuba

USS *Hecuba* (AKS-12)

USS Hecuba (AKS-12) was an *Acubens*-class general stores issue ship commissioned by the U.S. Navy for service in World War II. She was responsible for delivering and disbursing goods and equipment to locations in the war zone.

Hecuba (AKS-12), originally Liberty ship SS *George W. Cable*, was launched by Delta Shipbuilding Co., New Orleans, Louisiana, 6 November 1944 under Maritime Commission contract; sponsored by Mrs. J. Alfred Chard; acquired and converted to Navy use at Todd-Johnson Drydocks Corp.; and commissioned 21 April 1945, Comdr. N. H. Castle in command.

World War II service

Following her conversion to a stores ship and shakedown training, *Hecuba* departed New Orleans, Louisiana, 31 May 1945 for duty in the Pacific Ocean, arriving Pearl Harbor 22 June. From Hawaii she sailed to the western Pacific, commencing her first issue to the fleet after her arrival at Eniwetok 16 July.

History	
United States	
Ordered:	as SS *George W. Cable* EC2-S-C1 hull
Laid down:	date unknown
Launched:	6 November 1944
Acquired:	date unknown
Commissioned:	21 April 1945
Decommissioned:	26 March 1947
Stricken:	date unknown
Fate:	sold for scrapping, 19 October 1964
General characteristics	
Displacement:	4,023 t.(lt) 14,350 t.(fl)
Length:	441 ft 7 in (134.59 m)
Beam:	56 ft 11 in (17.35 m)
Draught:	27 ft 7 in (8.41 m)
Propulsion:	reciprocating steam engine, single shaft, 2,500 hp
Speed:	11 knots (20 km/h)
Endurance:	17,000 miles
Complement:	195
Armament:	one 5 in (130 mm) dual purpose gun mount, one single 3 in (76 mm) dual purpose gun mount, eight single 20 mm gun mounts

Hecuba arrived back in Pearl Harbor 18 August to reload general supplies for ships of the fleet. She sailed to Ulithi, arriving 10 September, and continued issuing the vital stores at that atoll as well as at Leyte and Okinawa until 28 November 1945. *Hecuba* departed for San Francisco, California, for additional supplies, only to return to Pearl Harbor 8 February 1946.

Post-war decommissioning

She decommissioned at Pearl Harbor 26 March 1946 and was intended for use in the Pacific atomic tests of that summer, only to be towed to San Francisco, California, in 1947 and placed in the National Defense Reserve Fleet, Suisun Bay, California, where she remained until sold for scrapping to Schintzer Steel Products Co., Portland, Oregon, 19 October 1964.

References

This article incorporates text from the public domain Dictionary of American Naval Fighting Ships.

Appendix C: LCM Specifications

◄ **LANDING CRAFT, MECHANIZED (MARK 3)**   **LCM(3)**

Operational use	Designed to land one medium (30-ton) tank or motor vehicles directly on beach.
Description	Two designs are in use, the HIGGINS type constituting the majority. Recent changes include addition of machine guns and magnesyn compass, higher bulwark, and slight rearrangement aft.
Capacity	One 30-ton tank or 60,000 lb. of cargo, or 60 troops. BUREAU type (few in number) carries 120,000 lb. of cargo.
Endurance	850 miles @ 6¼ kts.; Speed, 8 kts. (loaded), 11 kts. 500 miles @ 7¼ kts.; (normal load). 140 miles @ full speed.
Dimensions	Length, 50'0" o. a. Beam, 14'1".
Displacement	Light, 52,000 lb. Draft, 3'0" for'd, 4'0" aft. Loaded, 52 tons.
Armament	Two .50-cal. M.G.
Armor	¼" HTS sides to control station. British are fitting bullet-proof mattresses.
Crew	4.
Propulsion	Two 110-225 hp. Diesels of different designs; twin screws.

◄ LCM(3) during trials. In the foreground the BUREAU type debarks a 30-ton General Grant tank. In the background is a HIGGINS design.

LCM(4), (5) and (7) are British models. See table for staff requirements.

◄ **LANDING CRAFT, MECHANIZED (MARK 6)**   **LCM(6)**

A Higgins type LCM(3) with 6' added to the hull amidships. Photo shows new portion unpainted. Other characteristics are similar to LCM(3).

LCM(3)

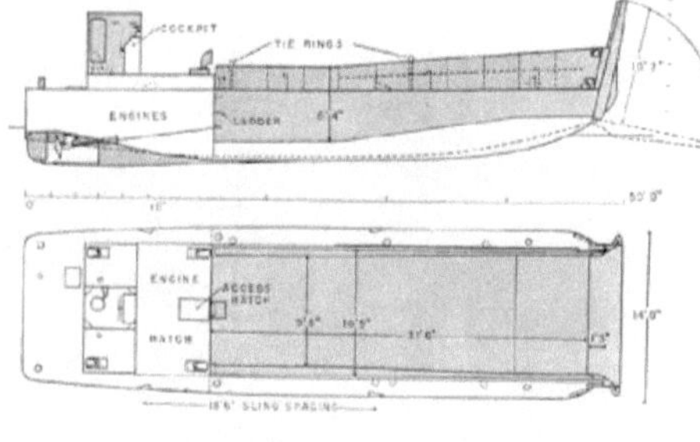

LCM

LIFTING RING
PILOT HOUSE
FUEL FILL
COWL VENT
ACCESS HATCH
VENT
CARGO SECURING RING
MANHOLES TO WING TANKS
CARGO TIE RING
ENGINE EXHAUST
RAMP HOIST CABLE
DECK PLATE
VENTS
CABLE GUARD
RAMP LATCH CABLE
MOORING BITT
CHOCK
RAMP LATCH

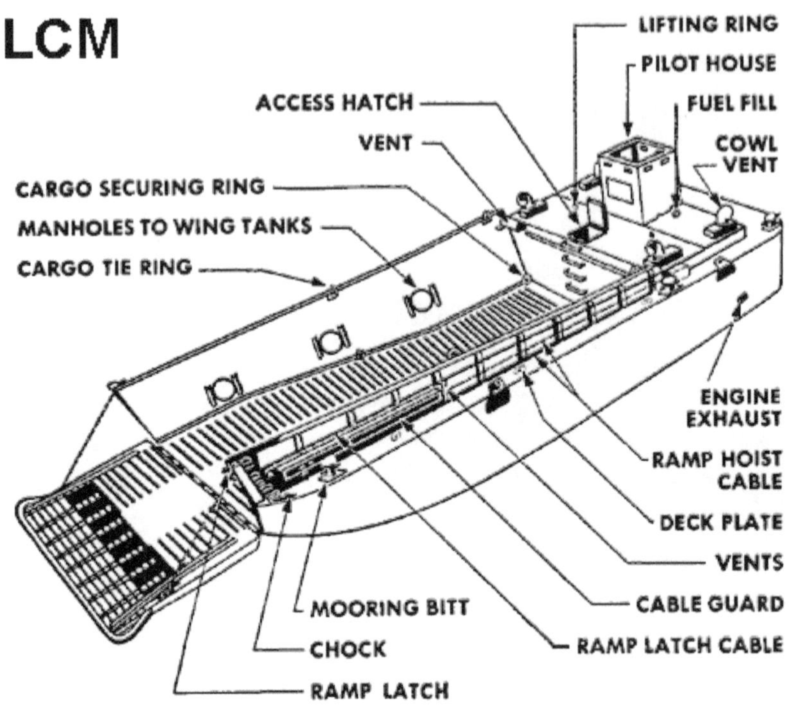

Appendix D: Map of the Hecuba's WWII Voyage

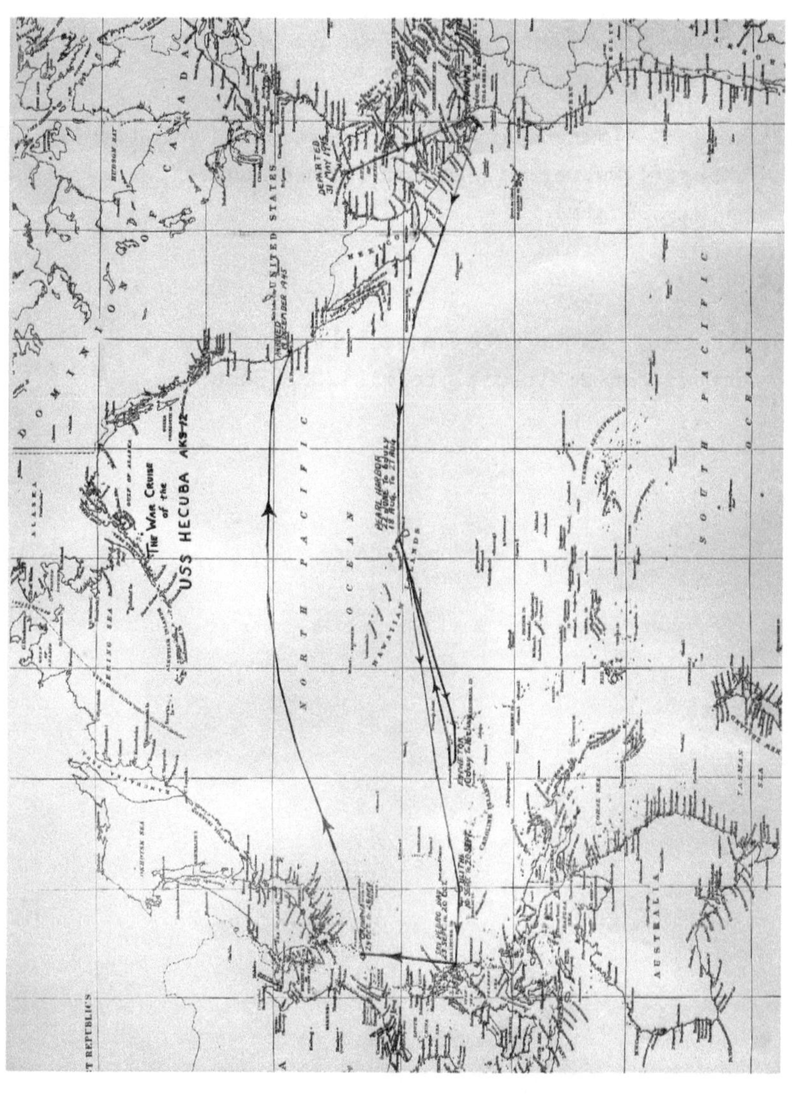

Bibliography

Appendix A

[1] Charles, Roland. *Troopships of World War II*. Washington DC: Army Transportation Association, 1947.

[2] Roger W Jordan, post to Warsailors.com, September 19, 2001, `https://www.warsailors.com/forum/archive/forum/read.php -1,91,399.html`.

Appendix B

[3] Wikipedia. 2007. "USS *Hecuba*." Last modified April 13, 2020. `https://en.wikipedia.org/wiki/USS_Hecuba`.

List of Images

Where not otherwise specified, images are taken from a personal collection.

The cover image is of the USS *Hecuba* and is credited as "Thompson Photo, Los Angeles."